Boris Pasternak

SELECTED POEMS

Boris Pasternak

✦

SELECTED
POEMS

TRANSLATED FROM THE RUSSIAN BY

JON STALLWORTHY

AND

PETER FRANCE

W · W · NORTON & COMPANY

New York / London

First American Edition 1983

Library of Congress Cataloging in Publication Data
Pasternak, Boris Leonidovich, 1890–1960.
   Selected poems.
   I. Stallworthy, Jon.   II. France, Peter, 1935–
III. Title.
PG3476.P27A276 1983b   891.71′42   83–8334

ISBN 0-393-01819-9

W. W. Norton & Company, Inc., 500 Fifth Avenue, New York, N. Y. 10110
W. W. Norton & Company Ltd., 37 Great Russell Street, London WC1B 3NU

1 2 3 4 5 6 7 8 9 0

Contents

Acknowledgements	9
Foreword by Y. B. Pasternak	11
Introduction	15

BEGINNINGS

It's February. Weeping, take ink	47
The sleepy garden scatters beetles	47
Venice	48

OVER THE BARRIERS

Winter Sky	53
The Urals for the First Time	53
Spring	54
Swifts	55
Improvisation	56
Marburg	56

MY SISTER LIFE

About These Poems	61
My sister, Life, is today overflowing	62
The Weeping Garden	63
Mirror	64
Rain	65
From Superstition	66

5

Oars Crossed   67
Spring Rain   67
Maladies of the Earth   68
Definition of Creativity   69
Sparrow Hills   70
Steppe   71
Storm, Instantaneous Forever   72
Let words drop, as resin   73

THEMES AND VARIATIONS

From Theme and Variations: Theme   77
Variation 3   78
Spring   78
January 1919   79
Thus they begin. At two they rush   80
Slanting pictures, streaming in   81

NINETEEN HUNDRED AND FIVE

Mutiny at Sea   85

POEMS OF VARIOUS YEARS

Putting Out to Sea   95
Lily of the Valley   96
Night Violet   97
Gathering Storm   98
To Anna Akhmatova   99
To a Friend   100

SECOND BIRTH

From Waves   103
Death of a Poet   104

Loving can be a heavy cross — 105
My beauty, all your symmetry — 105
No one will be in the house — 106
While we are climbing in the Caucasus — 107
If I had known that this is what happens — 109

ON EARLY TRAINS

From Summer Notes — 113
Pine Trees — 114
False Alarm — 116
Spring Again — 117
Winter Approaches — 118
The Old Park — 119
Fresco Come to Life — 121

POEMS FROM *Doctor Zhivago*

Hamlet — 125
In Holy Week — 125
Foul Ways in Spring — 128
The Wind — 129
Hops — 130
Wedding — 130
Autumn — 132
Winter Night — 133
August — 135
Magdalene — 137
The Garden of Gethsemane — 138

WHEN THE WEATHER CLEARS

In everything I want to reach — 143
July — 144
Hayricks — 145

When the Weather Clears   146
The Wind (*Four fragments about Blok*)   147
Snow Is Falling   150
After the Blizzard   152
It Has All Been Fulfilled   153
Nobel Prize   154

Notes   155

Acknowledgements

ACKNOWLEDGEMENTS are due to the editors of the following periodicals in which some of these translations first appeared: *Agenda, Critical Quarterly, Hudson Review, New England Review, Quarto, South-East Arts Review,* and *Vanderbilt Poetry Review.* 'Winter Approaches' and 'The Old Park' are reprinted by permission from *The Hudson Review,* vol. xxxiv, no. 4 (Winter 1981–2), copyright © 1982 by Jon Stallworthy and Peter France.

We are also grateful for the assistance and encouragement of many friends and colleagues, who commented on these translations and gave valuable help with the Introduction and Notes. In particular, we wish to thank Christopher Barnes, Ephim Fogel, Alexander Zholkovsky, and above all Yevgeny Borisovich Pasternak.

Foreword

IT is a flattering but difficult task to write a brief foreword to this selection of my father's poems translated by Jon Stallworthy and Peter France. The ideal epigraph for any book of poems would in my opinion be Fyodor Tyutchev's famous words: 'We cannot guess what echo our words will find, and sympathy is given to us like grace.' With poetry in translation, poetry at one remove, this sober scepticism is doubly in order. What is more, someone with a limited knowledge of the language is in no position to judge how Russian poetry sounds in contemporary English. For the twentieth-century European conception of verse is quite distinct from that of the nineteenth century, and Pasternak's poetic discoveries had almost nothing to do with the formal aspect of the art. This was no accident, for he was soon persuaded by his own experience that free verse was unnatural in the Slavonic languages, and in any case he was convinced that 'the most striking discoveries have been made when artists were so overwhelmed by their message that they had no time for reflection and hastened to say new things in the old language, not stopping to notice whether it was old or new'.*

Pasternak's views on literary translation were based on his own immense experience as a translator. Circumstances were such that for long periods of his life translation was his only source of income. Although he always considered it a task of secondary importance, and compared it with the work of an artist copying classical models in an art gallery, he nevertheless preferred it to all other ways of earning a living.

* 'People and Positions', *Novy Mir*, no. 1, 1967, p. 211.

Pasternak was always glad to learn that his poetry was being translated and published in another language, from the French translations of E. Izvolskaya in 1925 to the German versions of P. D. Keil and the English ones of Eugene Kayden in 1958. What pleased him was not so much the quality of the translations as the mere fact that people all over the world knew him and listened to him. He once wrote:

> Translations are pointless unless their link with the original is closer than is usually the case. Textual equivalence is too weak a link to guarantee the value of a translation. Translations of this kind do not deliver what they have promised. Their pale replicas give no idea of the essential feature of the objects which they attempt to reflect – their power. In order for a translation to achieve its aim, it must be tied to the original by a more real connection. The relation between the original and the translation must be that between foundation and building, between trunk and branches. The translation must be the work of an author who has felt the influence of the original long before he begins his work. It must be the fruit of the original, its historical consequence.
>
> More than this; we have said that translation is inconceivable because the principal charm of a work of art lies in its unrepeatability. How then can a translation repeat it? But translation *is* conceivable, because ideally it too will be a work of art; sharing a common text, it will stand alongside the original, unrepeatable in its own right. And translation is conceivable because for centuries before our time whole literatures have translated one another. Translation is not a method of getting to know isolated works, it is the channel whereby cultures and peoples communicate down the centuries.*

Pasternak brought into modern Russian literature Goethe's *Faust*, Shakespeare's most important tragedies and history plays, the lyric poetry of Byron, Shelley, Verlaine, Rilke, and the great Georgian poet Baratashvili – and much more besides. The volume of his translations is greater than that of his own collected works.

What enabled him to accomplish this great labour was his amazingly clear and untroubled feeling for the unity of human

---

* 'Notes of a Translator', *Znamya*, no. 1–2, 1944, pp. 165–6.

history and spiritual life. In his view this awareness was an essential quality of the generation whose childhood and youth belonged to those years which Russians long continued to call 'the time of peace' and which to a great extent corresponded to a certain notion of Edwardian England. Projecting his own memories on to the more distant age of Shakespeare, Pasternak said when introducing a public reading of his translation of *Henry IV*: 'This was what is called "good old merry England". It corresponded more or less to what we are thinking of when we talk about pre-war life. Shakespeare was an expression of faith in the fact that streets, taverns, houses, human habits, household objects, kitchen utensils and the like were all made by God much as he made the leaves on the trees, and that all this is entirely natural – just as some of us in childhood believed that even the railways were a part of nature.'*

Although it was possible to sense in the atmosphere of the beginning of the twentieth century the approach of the catastrophe which lent such tragic beauty to the poetry of Alexander Blok, this was still only a foreboding. The world of spiritual happenings was full of meaning and substance; lyrical self-expression and the interest of the artist in the details of his own personal biography and in the fate of a personality which was not defined by its place in the social hierarchy, all of this was considered entirely natural, as is evident in the painting of the Impressionists, the prose of Proust, and the poems of Rilke.

Everywhere one was aware of the presence of those older contemporaries: Tolstoy, Dostoyevsky, Ostrovsky, Chekhov, and the musicians and artists of the same generation. Their art and their moral teaching served as a measuring rod and indicated to the educated youth of the time what heights they must aim at.

Pasternak once compared the Renaissance and the early twentieth century in the following terms:

---

*From a record, *Shakespeare translated by S. Marshak and B. Pasternak*, Melodiya, 1979.

Our age has reached a new understanding of the aspect of the Gospels that has always been best understood and expressed by artists. It was strong in the Apostles and then it withered away in the Fathers, the Church, morality and politics ... It is the idea that the communion of mortals is immortal and that life is symbolic, because full of meaning.*

A broad education and the study of philosophy, history, and languages were thus no longer purely ancillary. They were a guarantee of the principle that was proclaimed at the dawn of European history, the truth which gives absolute significance to every single human being. All his life Pasternak remained true to this doctrine of love, trust and understanding between people as the only possible alternative to the unthinking and inflexible march to universal self-destruction.

Yevgeny Borisovich Pasternak

*From a note in the Pasternak family papers in Moscow.

Introduction

THIS book is the fruit of collaboration between friends. We
have worked together in the belief that by doing so we
could best do justice to Pasternak's poetry. Our method of working
is briefly outlined in the introduction to an earlier volume of trans-
lations from the Russian, Alexander Blok, *The Twelve and other
Poems* (Eyre & Spottiswoode, 1970; subsequently published as
Selected Poems in the Penguin Modern European Poets collection,
1974). There are those who question the wisdom of such joint efforts
and hold that a worthwhile translation must be the work of one
person only. It seems pointless to debate such questions in the
abstract, and we can only set before the reader the results of our
work. Our aim has been to produce English poems which convey
the sense of the Russian originals and something of their formal
qualities. Throughout his poetic career Pasternak wrote in-
novatively in traditional forms, and we have tried to reflect this
tension, while striving above all to convey his pristine vision of
the world.

Pasternak is principally known to English-speaking readers as
the author of *Doctor Zhivago*. We have attempted to offer a
representative selection of his poetry of all periods from 1912 to
1959. Like many modern Russian poets, he thought of his poems
as forming 'cycles' or 'books', rather than as isolated units. Strictly
speaking, therefore, one should translate and read them in this way.
My Sister Life, for instance, is given 'chapter headings' and contains
at least a hint of narrative development, while the Zhivago poems,
which form the last chapter of the novel, make up a dynamic unity
in which the movement of the seasons echoes the story of Christ.
Even so, Pasternak himself sanctioned the printing of selections from

his poetry, many of the poems first appeared separately in journals, and there is no doubt that a poem such as 'Hamlet' can be taken out of the context of *Doctor Zhivago* and still remain rich and powerful.

There is some excellent critical writing on Pasternak in English, notably Henry Gifford's *Pasternak* (Cambridge University Press, 1977) and the two collections of essays – each also entitled *Pasternak* – edited respectively by Donald Davie and Angela Livingstone (Modern Judgements, Macmillan, 1969) and by Victor Erlich (Twentieth-Century Views, Prentice-Hall, 1978). Both of the latter contain the fine essay by Andrey Sinyavsky, which first appeared as the introduction to the best Soviet edition of Pasternak's poems. So rather than write another critical introduction, we thought it better to offer the reader an account of the poet's life, his artistic aims, and his principal writings. In this context, many of the poems take on a fuller meaning than if they are read in isolation.

Much of what we know about Pasternak's life comes from his own autobiographical writings, *Safe Conduct* (1931) and the more laconic *Essay in Autobiography* (1956), both of which have appeared in more than one English translation, as well as from his fiction and verse. Many people who knew him well are still alive and have a great deal to say about so memorable a person; in the way of written sources one should mention the memoirs of his brother Alexander (shortly to be published in English by Oxford University Press) and of various people who knew him, including Alexander Gladkov (*Meetings with Pasternak*, translated by M. Hayward, Collins and Harvill Press, 1977) and Olga Ivinskaya (*A Captive of Time*, translated by M. Hayward, Collins and Harvill Press, 1978). In addition he left a voluminous correspondence, much of which has not yet been published. Because of the mass of relevant material and its dispersal in Russia and abroad, there is not yet a good full-scale biography of the poet, but the main outlines of his career are clear enough.

In 1927 Pasternak wrote: 'I am the son of an artist, and I came to know art and great men and women from my childhood on.

I grew to regard the lofty and the exceptional as natural; from the time of my birth such things were fused with everyday life in my experience of society.' He was indeed born into a favoured milieu, the cultural and intellectual elite of Moscow in the decades before the Revolution of 1917. His father, Leonid Pasternak, was an important painter, the illustrator of Tolstoy's *Resurrection* and from 1905 a member of the Academy of Arts. He was a natural draughtsman, his pencil was constantly with him, and his many sketches and paintings give a vivid idea of the world in which the young Boris grew up.

The poet's mother, Roza Kaufman, was a brilliant pianist who had won a European reputation by the age of twenty. After some highly acclaimed concert seasons, she virtually gave up playing in public so as to devote more time and energy to her family, and she helped to create round her children a rich and happy atmosphere. At the same time she continued to work as a teacher at the Moscow Conservatoire and to play the piano for several hours a day, and composers such as Scriabin and Rachmaninov would bring her their latest work to play.

Boris Pasternak, the oldest child in the family, was born in Moscow in 1890. When he was four years old his father was invited to teach at the School of Painting, Sculpture and Architecture, and the family moved into an apartment at the school which was to be Boris's permanent childhood home. Here there were constant visits from prominent Moscow writers, artists and intellectuals, and sometimes there were family concerts. Pasternak later dated the beginning of his conscious life from the evening in November 1894 when he was woken by the sound of Tchaikovsky's Piano Trio being played in the next room for Lev Tolstoy and other friends of the family. From time to time the Pasternaks went abroad (thus to Berlin for a year in 1906) and they received many foreign visitors, for instance, the as yet unknown Rainer Maria Rilke who was a guest in 1899 and whose writing was to exert a great influence on the young Boris.

Pasternak's autobiographical writing, like his poetry, is alive with the feeling of the family home, family holidays, and indeed of the whole city of Moscow, poised as it was between the old and the new. It is clear that his childhood environment developed in him a vivid sensual awareness of the world around him, and this provided the basis for his striking ability to paint from nature. In later years he gave this the name of 'subjective-biographical realism', and it lay at the heart of his aesthetic. At the same time, the family's way of life developed in him the habit of regular work, so that at the age of seventy he could say with satisfaction that, unbelievable as it might seem, there had not been a single wasted day in his life.

Apart from his parents, Boris's first teachers were private tutors; then, in 1901, he entered the Fifth Moscow *Gymnasium* (high school), which gave a predominantly classical education. He later said that his whole generation was characterized by 'the breadth of their general artistic gifts, with a particular leaning to the fine arts and music'. He himself drew well (which pleased his father), his first enthusiasm was botany, but from the age of thirteen he devoted himself above all to music. In this he was greatly influenced by the composer Scriabin, who was a friend of the family and their holiday neighbour during the summer of 1903. The impression made by Scriabin's music is strikingly evoked in *Safe Conduct*, and the composer was to remain for Pasternak an example of inspired artistry. Encouraged by him, he devoted much of the next six years to the study of composition, following courses at the Conservatoire. Three finished piano pieces as well as numerous exercises in harmony and counterpoint have survived from these years.

It was assumed by everyone that Pasternak would become a professional musician, but he himself was uneasy at the prospect, partly, according to the *Essay in Autobiography*, because of his lack of technical skill. In 1909 he decided to give up any plans for a musical career and entered the Law Faculty at Moscow University. Very soon, however, he transferred to philosophy, to which he devoted himself whole-heartedly. In the summer of 1912 he spent a term at the University of Marburg in Germany, working under the neo-Kantian Hermann Cohen. He gave successful papers at university seminars there, and the door now seemed open to an academic career, but instead, partly it seems under the stress of an unhappy love affair (see the poem 'Marburg'), he gave up philosophy, just as he had earlier given up music, and at last found his true calling, poetry. He had in fact been writing poems and prose for some years, probably since 1909, but he had had doubts about his literary vocation, keeping what he wrote to himself and trying to abstain from writing. From 1912 onwards his road was clear.

None of Pasternak's youthful enthusiasms was wasted. His poetry and prose bear the mark of his precocious artistic sensibility and of his passion for music. At the same time his philosophical training can be felt in his desire and ability to see the general in the particular (as, for instance, in the poem beginning 'In everything I want to reach') and in the discipline he imposes on his spontaneous vividness of sensation. Moreover, to judge from his writings and conversations, it was in his student years that he formed many of the ideas and attitudes which were to help him to live through the hard years that followed. He learned for instance to live without hoarding and not to worry about losing things. 'It is more important in life to lose than to acquire,' he wrote in the *Essay in Autobiography*. 'The grain will not sprout unless first it dies. One must remain untiringly alive, looking into the future and feeding on the living reserves which memory and oblivion together accumulate.'

A particularly important idea which we can date from this period is 'the idea of history as a second universe created by humanity, with the aid of time and memory, in response to the fact of death'. It is significant that in recalling his visit to Italy in *Second Birth* he writes first of all:

I loved the living essence of historical symbolism, in other words the instinct which has enabled us, like house martins, to build a world, an immense nest made of earth and sky, of life and death, and of two kinds of time, time present and time absent. I understood that it was saved from disintegration by the cohesive force contained in the transparently figurative quality of every particle of it.

Because he felt so deeply the inexhaustible richness of the European historical tradition, Pasternak, though himself a highly original writer, never seems to have felt any great desire for novelty as such, and subsequently he often expressed his distrust for what he saw as the gratuitious search for the new. His own idea of art always centred on content and meaning.

His feeling for history also freed him from the need to impose his ideas on other people. An indication of this can be found in the tolerant traditionalism of what he says about the Bible in *Safe Conduct*:

> I understand that the Bible, for instance, is not so much a book with a definitive text as the notebook of humanity and that everything lasting is like this. It is a living thing not when it is an enforced doctrine but when it is receptive to all the analogies that successive centuries make with it. I understand that the history of culture is a chain of figurative equations, in which an unknown new element is brought into relation with what is already known; the known, which remains constant, is the legend on which tradition is founded, whereas the unknown, which is constantly new, is the present moment in the evolution of the culture.

These words were written in 1930, during the heyday of atheism and materialism, when the mere mention of the Bible in print was liable to be considered dangerously anachronistic.

To judge from the *Essay in Autobiography*, Pasternak attached particular importance among his youthful theoretical writings to a paper on 'Symbolism and Immortality', which dates from February 1917. The text has not survived, but it apparently concerned the immortality of the individual soul as a part of the spiritual life of mankind, a life which is accumulated over the centuries out of the experience of every spiritual being. This aspect of human history is particularly evident in art. Summing up his paper in the *Essay in Autobiography*, Pasternak concludes:

> Although the artist is of course mortal like everyone else, the joy of existence experienced by him is immortal and can be experienced by other people centuries later, since his work allows them to come close to the living, personal form of his original sensations.

Apart from their political significance, the years preceding the Revolution were also a time of great intellectual and artistic richness in Russia. Since the turn of the century or before, the country had been enjoying a philosophical and religious revival in which the symbolist poets played a leading part; it was a time of endless meetings, lectures, and debates in which great and exciting ideas were elaborated, attacked, and defended. In the arts the Russian avant-garde was closely linked to new movements in Western Europe; this was the age of Kandinsky, Chagall, Malevich and Larionov, of Scriabin and Stravinsky, of Diaghilev, Meyerhold and Stanislavsky.

As far as poetry was concerned, the great poet of the age was Alexander Blok, whose influence and significance for the younger generation is described by Pasternak in his autobiographical writings and in *Doctor Zhivago*; in the *Essay in Autobiography* he writes:

> I spent my youth under the influence of Blok, as did many of my contemporaries. . . . He had all the qualities which go to make a great poet – fire, tenderness, insight, his own conception of the world, his own gift of transforming everything he touched, his own reserved, restrained, self-effacing destiny.

Blok was a Symbolist (though such labels are very inadequate) and in the first decade of the twentieth century the Symbolists had been the dominant movement in Russian poetry. From about 1910, however, as the great generation which included Anna Akhmatova, Boris Pasternak, Osip Mandelstam, Marina Tsvetaeva, and Vladimir Mayakovsky came of age, the Symbolist hegemony was challenged by other movements, notably the neo-classical Acmeists and the much more avant-garde Futurists.

In the ferment of the time, short-lived groups were formed in haste and pooled their resources or found patrons to publish their work. In 1913 a new group called 'Lirika' brought out a volume of writing which contained Pasternak's first published work, a group of five poems (including 'It's February. Weeping, take ink' and 'The sleepy garden scatters beetles'). The following year another more innovatory, Futurist group called 'Centrifuga' split off from 'Lirika' and poems and articles by Pasternak also appeared in two volumes published by this movement. It would be wrong, however, to think that this brief association with 'Centrifuga' made him a 'futurist' poet; such literary groupings were not essential to him and as the years went by he spoke with increasing regret about his connection with them.

Pasternak's first published poems did not attract a great deal of attention, though the Symbolist leader Valery Bryusov gave them a brief but favourable mention in one of his surveys of recent writing. Of his pre-war poems, which were first collected in a volume called *Twin in the Clouds* (1914), Pasternak later selected about a third to make up the opening section of his complete poems, 'Beginnings' (many of these, like all his earlier poems, were considerably reworked over the years). In the *Essay in Autobiography*, distinguishing his poems from those of Mayakovsky with their 'tonal and rhetorical effects', he stressed that from the beginning what mattered to him was *content*:

> My abiding dream was that the poem itself should contain something, a new thought or a new image.... This is how it was when I wrote the poem entitled 'Venice'. What I saw before me as I wrote was the city built on water, the figures of eight and circles of its reflections drifting and multiplying, swelling up like a biscuit in tea.... I did not want anything to come from myself, from the reader or from the theory of art. I just wanted [this] poem to contain the city of Venice.

The notion that poetry or literature should 'contain' reality is a constant in Pasternak's aesthetic thinking (see 'Spring', p. 54, and 'In everything I want to reach', p. 143).

The spring and summer of 1914 were marked for the poet by a powerful awareness of the imminent end of a time of peace and stability, a time when the experience of the individual human being seemed the main thing in life and when, in his words, it was easier and more natural to love anything on earth than to hate it. He spent the summer and autumn of this year near Aleksin on the river Oka (some eighty miles south of Moscow) as a tutor in the household of the Symbolist poet Yurgis Baltrushaytis. Baltrushaytis was at this time the literary director of the newly founded Kamerny

Theatre in Moscow, and it was at his request that Pasternak translated for the theatre Kleist's *Der Zerbrochene Krug*.

The outbreak of war found Pasternak on the Oka, and in his letters of this time his descriptions of the people's grief foreshadow his later treatment of this theme in prose and verse. He himself was unable to serve in the army, as a childhood fall from a horse had left him with one leg shorter than the other. Much of the time between 1914 and 1917 he spent as a clerk at a chemical works in the Ural Mountains far to the east of Moscow (see 'The Urals for the First Time'). This prolonged period away from the city was a productive one for him. In February 1917 he wrote a letter to his father describing his current work and his literary plans:

> I am writing all sorts of things at the moment, going from one thing to another. I am writing a book of stories. Poems too.... And I also want to write a book of essays. You know, the sort of thing I sometimes talk about – art, or great men, or the fact that living feelings, the kind that tangibly pervade the world of human beings, as airy vapours penetrate overgrown gardens and meadows in summer, at midday, after a thunderstorm, that such feelings, which everyone carries within himself and embodies in his own life, are entrusted to the care of all mankind.

The 'book of stories' was probably intended to consist of three pieces, one of which ('The Line of Apelles') was published in 1925, while the other two remained unfinished. The book of essays was written over the next two years and included pieces about Kleist and Shakespeare (never printed and subsequently lost) and an essay, 'Quintessentia', which was a kind of artistic manifesto and was printed four years later under the title 'A Few Theses'. The planned volume may have also included 'Dialogue' (a dramatic fragment in prose printed in 1918) and 'Letters from Tula', a story about the responsibility of the artist, printed in 1922. At about the same time he also wrote some reviews of new poetry, but these never appeared.

As for his own poetry, Pasternak composed two volumes of verse in the war years. One of them was destroyed in a fire in 1915. The other was published in 1917 as *Over the Barriers*, a title retained by the author for considerably revised and enlarged collections issued in 1929 and 1931. He himself later defined *Over the Barriers* in the following terms:

> From being the name of a book, it became the name of a period or manner, and I subsequently grouped together under this title pieces which were written in later years, if they were similar in character to this first book, i.e. if they were marked by objectivity of theme and the rapid pictorial representation of movement.

(In the present volume only poems of the earlier period appear under the heading 'Over the Barriers'; the later ones are included in 'Poems of Various Years', the title finally preferred by their author.)

The war years were therefore fruitful for Pasternak's work and saw the formation of some of his characteristic traits as a writer. In addition, these months of solitary life in the provinces confirmed him in what one might call his artistic asceticism, the determination to cultivate tendencies which were valuable for his writing and to suppress those which were detrimental to it. From this time on he often spoke of himself as an instrument which must be kept in tune, writing for instance that 'the one thing that is in our power is not to distort the voice of life which sounds within us'.

An immediate consequence of this was that he gradually cut himself off from aesthetic schools and movements and that he rejected what he called in *Safe Conduct* the 'romantic manner', by which he meant principally the insistence on the 'I' of the writer, who is set off in a spectacular way against the mass of ordinary people. In particular he distanced himself from the Futurists, whose eye-catching public appearances dominated the Russian literary and artistic scene in the years preceding the Revolution. One of the Futurist leaders was the young Vladimir Mayakovsky, whom Pasternak first met in 1914. The two poets admired one another intensely; Pasternak later wrote of their first meeting: 'I liked the author no less than his verse'. Because of his delight in Mayakovsky's poetry, however, he felt the need to pursue his own separate path: 'In order to avoid repeating him or seeming to imitate him,

I repressed those tendencies in myself which echoed his – the heroic tone, which in my case would have been false, and the striving for effect. This disciplined and purified my style.' Later, when Mayakovsky became the 'drummer of the Revolution', Pasternak found himself more and more at odds with him, and when Mayakovsky finally shot himself in 1930 (see 'Death of a Poet'), he became for Pasternak the tragic example of what awaits a poet who gives himself over to romantic innovation in order to satisfy his allies and his public. By contrast, Pasternak was always to stress the responsibility and the modesty of the artist.

At the time of the February Revolution of 1917, Pasternak was still in the Urals, and he immediately set out for Moscow. The period between the February and October Revolutions was to be a central theme in his later work. Describing his feelings at this time in the afterword to *Safe Conduct*, he wrote:

I have not really been able to give a proper account of those eternally first days of all revolutions, when the Camille Desmoulins of this world leap on to tables and set passers-by alight with their toasts to the air. I was a witness to such days. Reality, like a natural daughter, ran half-dressed out of confinement and set her whole self, illegitimate and un-dowered from head to foot, against legitimate history. I saw summer on the earth, and it seemed unable to recognize itself; it was natural and pre-historic, as in a revelation. I wrote a book about it, and in this book I expressed all the most unprecedented and intangible things that can be known about a revolution.

This is a reference to *My Sister Life*, one of the peaks of Pasternak's poetic achievement. It is a book about revolution, but it is also a book about private life, and in an oblique way it follows the course of a love affair. All its short poems are welded together into one single easy movement, and any poems of 1917 which did not fit into it went into a more miscellaneous collection, *Themes and Variations*. In the circumstances of the Civil War, neither of these books could be published for five years, but both became widely known in manuscript.

When *My Sister Life* was eventually published in 1922, it immediately won Pasternak a place among the leading writers of the time. He felt this as a liberation from any kind of dependence. 'When *My Sister Life* appeared, expressing completely uncontemporary sides of poetry which had been revealed to me in the revolutionary summer, I did not care at all what the power was called to which I owed this book, because it was immeasurably greater than me and the poetic theories surrounding me', he later wrote in *Safe Conduct*. This rejection of narrow topicality is characteristic of Pasternak. He saw in tradition a continuing conversation which is carried on down the ages. As opposed to derivative writers or mere innovators, the great writers are for him discoverers of new spiritual realms. They symbolize the age they live in, and their work becomes a part of this unceasing conversation, to which they add their own inimitable voices.

From about the same period as *My Sister Life* and *Themes and Variations* one can also date the long story 'The Childhood of Luvers', Pasternak's most important piece of fiction before *Doctor Zhivago*, which in some respects it prefigures. Then, in the hungry years between 1918 and 1921, he was obliged to work hard as a translator; producing among other things, versions of plays by Kleist and Ben Jonson, poems by Hans Sachs, Goethe, Harwegh, Charles van Lerberghe, and the German Expressionists. None of this work is comparable to his great achievements as a translator in the second half of his life.

As Henry Gifford writes in his book about Pasternak, 'the revolution of October 1917 drove iron wedges into the national life, between one class and another, between the past and the future, and between the sensibility of one generation – Pasternak's own – and that of its successor'. Many members of the upper and middle classes went abroad, including many writers and artists. Indeed, sooner or later all were obliged to choose between emigrating and living with the new Bolshevik order. Pasternak was far from sharing Mayakovsky's enthusiastic acceptance of the Revolution, but he, like Anna Akhmatova and Osip Mandelstam for instance, stayed in Russia – at the end of his life he was to fight desperately to avoid exile. Most of his family, however, left Russia. In 1921 Leonid

Pasternak with his wife and daughters went for lengthy medical treatment to Germany, and although they retained Russian citizenship they never returned and eventually settled in England.

Their two sons, Boris and Alexander, remained behind, living in an overcrowded communal flat in Moscow. At the beginning of 1922, Boris Pasternak was married to Yevgeniya Lurye, who was at this time a student at the Art Institute. They spent the second half of that year and the beginning of 1923 with his parents in Berlin. This turned out to be their last meeting, in spite of the fact that nearly every year he applied unsuccessfully for permission to visit them.

On their return to Moscow, the young couple had many worries. All their belongings were crowded into a single large room, and things became even more difficult after the birth of their son Evgeny in 1923. The gifted and highly strung Yevgeniya Pasternak was devoted to her work as an artist, and she and her husband had to work at night. Although gradually Pasternak was able to publish more, they never had enough money. But such material difficulties were not the principal cause of the oppression which he felt from the early 1920s. Much more serious were the problems of writing lyric poetry in a new age.

It is true that he continued to write fine short poems at this time, many of them being addressed to friends and contemporaries whose fate touched on his own or concerned him (see, for instance, 'To Anna Akhmatova'). These pieces were included in *Themes and Variations* and in the second edition of *Over the Barriers*, but they did not satisfy Pasternak. Like many of his contemporaries he was beginning to experience a feeling of tragedy. The old peaceful order in which the lyric poet could work with security and confidence had been replaced by a world of destruction and antagonism. In this world the time-honoured themes of lyric poetry – the individual and his or her inner feelings – had lost the soil in which they flourished; it seemed that the world was once again, as in pagan times, receptive only to myth and epic. Gradually Pasternak came to believe that the poet and the artist in general had no assured place in society and could only live as outsiders. Creation had now to be seen in the light of a moral duty, which obliged the poet to sacrifice his career to posterity, the immediate to the eternal. He wrote about this in a letter of 1929:

> Contemporary life does not offer the lyric poet a common language or anything else. It merely tolerates him, in a kind of extraterritoriality. That is why this kind of writing no longer has a place in present-day aesthetics. The general tone of expression these days is no longer set by the lyric poet, nor by the predominance of one kind of real-life impression over another, it has become a kind of moral question. In other words, where in healthier times we considered it *natural* to talk in this or that way, we now (each in his own way) consider it to be our *duty*.

In the light of such views, one can understand how Pasternak was brought to the sacrificial view of the artist's calling which is central to his later writing.

The effort involved in attempting to write and the importance for Pasternak of remaining faithful to his past is well seen in the following passage from a letter to Mandelstam, written when he was starting to work on his verse novel *Spektorsky* in 1925:

> This is a return to the old poetic rails of a train which was derailed and had been lying at the bottom of an embankment for six years, a train which included *My Sister Life*, 'Luvers' and some parts of *Themes and Variations*... Since the beginning of January I have been working in bursts, a bit at a time. It is terribly difficult. Everything is rusty, broken, unscrewed, covered with encrusted layers of superficial insensitivity, deafness and dull routine. It's disgusting – but at least my work is far removed from the present day, just as it was at the time of our first literary efforts, our joyful labours. Do you remember? That is the charm of it. It reminds me of forgotten things, gives new life to powers which seemed exhausted. The illusion of the extraordinariness of the epoch vanishes. The eschatological style (the end of an age, the end of the revolution, the end of youth, the collapse of Europe) sinks back between its banks and grows shallower until it ceases to flow. The fate of culture (in inverted commas) becomes once again as in the old days a matter of choice and good will. Things finish only if they are allowed to finish. It is premature to look for the end of all the things I have listed. And so I return to unfinished business. Not as a celebrity or a literary man. Not as a special kind of person. No, simply as a civilian, a normal happy-or-unhappy, unobtrusive, unknown person.

Even so, Pasternak felt that the time called for epic writing and he turned to historical subjects. In 1923 he wrote 'Lofty Malady' and between 1925 and 1927 the long poems *1905* and *Lieutenant Schmidt*, which describe heroes and events of the first Russian revolution of 1905 (see 'Mutiny at Sea'). He was encouraged by Marina Tsvetaeva, who had gone abroad; the two poets had never met, but they admired one another immensely (the *Essay in Autobiography* includes an important section on Tsvetaeva) and corresponded with one another. Pasternak sent her the newly completed chapters of his long poems and dedicated *Lieutenant Schmidt* to her. Throughout the second half of the 1920s his main occupation was the verse novel *Spektorsky* (published in 1931). Together with the thematically related prose work entitled 'A Tale' (1929), this contains the essential elements of his writing of this period; both link the private destinies of an ordinary individual (albeit a writer) with the greatest historical events of the time, war and revolution.

As the twenties progressed, it became apparent to many that post-Revolutionary hopes for the restoration of the shattered fabric of society and the return to peaceful productive life were not being realized. In the late twenties came a new wave of intolerance and terror. Lenin had died in 1924, and Stalin eventually emerged victorious from the struggle for succession in 1928. Trotsky was driven into exile and official nonexistence, and one after another all of Stalin's potential rivals were to be eliminated. After the relatively tolerant period of the New Economic Policy, there was a clamp-down in all fields, including the literary world; eventually, in 1932, the doctrine of Socialist Realism was proclaimed, and the Writers' Union became the sole guardian of orthodoxy.

Above all, the years around 1930 were the years of the first Five-Year Plan and of the forced collectivization of Soviet agriculture, which involved the elimination of the rich peasants (*kulaks*), the removal of entire populations, a considerable increase in the flow of labour to the camps, and a renewed wave of food shortages in the cities. It was a time of crisis, as Pasternak was well aware. In January 1930 he wrote to his parents:

29

Everyone is living under very great pressure at the moment, but the weight oppressing the city-dwellers is quite simply a *privilege* compared with what is going on in the countryside. Things of immense and lasting significance are being done there, and you would need to be blind not to see the unheard-of prospects which this promises the nation, but I also think that you have to be a peasant to *dare* talk about it, in other words you have to have been at the receiving end of this massive surgery. To sing about it from the sidelines is even more immoral than to write about war from the rear. This is what the air is full of.

This then is the background to such poems as 'To a Friend', which speaks of the difficulty of coming to terms with a new order that might perhaps 'promise unheard-of prospects', but at an unheard-of cost. In Pasternak's milieu many felt the temptation of suicide at this time. For the poet it was essential to overcome this temptation and the fear of what the future held in store, and to continue working when lyricism, art, and even spiritual existence had no longer any secure place in society. He expressed all this through the metaphor of 'second birth', which appears in his writings in 1928.

It is interesting in this respect to look at the reworking of the early poem 'Marburg'. In the first version (1916), Pasternak stressed the idea of the newness of life and his amazement, as if he were newly born into this brave new world. On revising the poem in 1928, he included the words: 'I could be counted among the *twice-born*', thus emphasizing the tragic motif of parting with the world on the threshold of suicide and overcoming this temptation in the name of a commitment to art. A further elaboration of this theme occurs in the prose work *Safe Conduct*, dedicated to the memory of Rilke, who was for Pasternak the incarnation of contemporary European lyric poetry. The death of the German poet came as a great shock to him. When he heard of it, he wrote to Marina Tsvetaeva on 3 February 1927:

Do you realize in all its starkness the degree to which you and I have been left orphans? No, I don't think you do, and it's just as well. The full blast of hopelessness diminishes a human being. I seem to be deprived of all aim in life. We must live for a long time now, a long life of sorrow – that is my duty, and yours too.

Safe Conduct was originally to be about Rilke, but in 1928 Pasternak wrote:

At first my main concern was to write about this amazing lyric poet ... but as I worked, the article I had planned turned itself into a series of autobiographical fragments about the formation and basis of my ideas about art. I have not yet thought of a title for this work, which I dedicate to his memory. It is not yet complete.

In fact he only set about completing it two years later and finally brought it to a conclusion in 1931. Meanwhile, in the spring of 1930, Mayakovsky had shot himself (see 'Death of a Poet') and under the shock of this tragic event Pasternak devoted much of the second and third parts of *Safe Conduct* to meditations on the fate of art and the artist. At about the same time, in the summer of 1930, he wrote the first poems in the collection *Second Birth*, which was to be a poetic declaration of his new position, as well as bearing the marks of a crisis and a new beginning in his private life.

Pasternak's mother-in-law had recently died after a serious illness, and Yevgeniya Pasternak herself was left in bad health; it was thought that in addition to anaemia and nervous trouble there had been a recurrence of the tuberculosis she had had as a child. In May 1930 her husband tried to get permission for a long visit abroad with his family, but was unsuccessful. So in the summer of that year the Pasternaks spent the holiday period near Kiev with the families of the philosopher Valentin Asmus and the pianist Genrikh Neuhaus, who was giving recitals in the city. It was Neuhaus's active and enterprising wife Zinaida who was mainly responsible for organizing this holiday, and Pasternak was won over by her beauty and her strength of character.

Then in the winter of 1930, with the help of Romain Rolland, permission was obtained for Yevgeniya Pasternak to go abroad with her son for medical treatment. The following spring they left for Germany. Pasternak thought that after treatment she would go on to study in Paris and pursue the artistic career she dreamed of. But less than a year later she returned to Moscow. Meanwhile, after his family's departure, Pasternak went to Kiev to meet Zinaida

Neuhaus and together they went to Georgia. It is to her that the beautiful love poems of *Second Birth* are addressed, and eventually, in 1934, she became his second wife.

In *Second Birth*, perhaps the most important poem is 'Waves' which was inspired by impressions of the Caucasus and Georgia. Travel descriptions here serve to express a philosophy of clarity, certitude and simplicity. This is how Pasternak puts it in the most famous lines of the poem:

> There is in the work of great poets
> Such naturalness that, when you come
> To recognize and know it,
> You can only be struck dumb.
>
> Aware of your kinship with all things,
> The future in what you can see,
> You fall, as into heresy,
> Into newfound simplicity.
>
> However, we shall not be spared
> Unless we conceal our hand.
> Though people need nothing so much,
> Complexity they understand.

Pasternak seems at this time to have been capable of more hope than Mandelstam, for instance, but he was fully aware that the path he was choosing was hazardous and that aesthetic considerations must be subordinated to the artist's sense of duty. All this is expressed in the famous poem 'If I had known that this is what happens' with its final stanza:

> When feeling dictates your lines,
> You step out, like a slave, to pace
> The stage, and here art stops,
> And earth and fate breathe in your face.

It was possible to suffer for dissidence in the 1920s, but in the thirties even a purely apolitical position came to be seen as a dangerous manifestation of independence. In poems and speeches of this period Pasternak continually defended the autonomy of the artist against those who wanted to enrol him in the troops of the revolution. He made a clear statement of his apolitical position in a proposed second edition of *Safe Conduct*, but this was suppressed after creating a scandal. At the same time a planned edition of his complete works was reduced to a single volume of selected poems, which was printed in 1933. The authorities were still willing to publish his poems, but not his prose.

If forced silence and victimization were a constant threat at this time, so was official favour. Pasternak feared that after Mayakovsky's death he might be made an official bard of the Soviet regime. Particularly around the time of the writers' congress of 1934, critics praised his poetic gifts to the skies, while at the same time offering him edifying advice designed to make him the kind of poet they wanted. Much later, in a private letter of 1953, he wrote of the agonies of this period and of his unsuccessful attempts to write a large-scale prose work:

At that time I was nineteen years younger, Mayakovsky had not yet been deified, they kept making a fuss of me and sending me on foreign trips, I could have written any filth or trash and they would have published it; I was not in fact suffering from any disease, but I was constantly unhappy and was pining away like a fairy-tale hero under the spell of an evil spirit. I wanted to write something honest and genuine in honour of the society which was so kind to me, but this would only have been possible if I had been willing to write something false. It was an insoluble problem like squaring the circle, and I was thrashing around in an uncertainty of intention which clouded every horizon and blocked every road.

In order to avoid the role that was being forced upon him (a role that he described as 'thrice-decorated wizard-consultant for poetry'), Pasternak was driven to take considerable risks. He not only gave his support to Lili Brik when she complained that Mayakovsky's memory was being neglected, he also wrote a special letter to Stalin thanking him for the decision to immortalize Mayakovsky as the greatest Soviet poet, thus saving him, Pasternak, from the fateful role that was being thrust upon him. At congresses and meetings of the Writers' Union he made public statements which although tactful were nevertheless firm in their resistance to the prevailing current. In 1936, for instance, in a speech on the subject of 'Modesty and Boldness' he told his fellow writers: 'On [the] themes that are common to us all I shall not speak in the common language; I am not going to repeat you, comrades, I am going to dispute with you.' At first the authorities tried to ignore such declarations, but gradually he began to be more openly criticized. Finally, after two provocative speeches by Pasternak at a discussion on formalism, and the publication of a cycle of poems called 'The Artist' in which he reiterated his position, the head of the Writers' Union referred to him as a traitor in a speech to the Congress of Soviets. From then on, he was no longer called on to play an active part in public affairs.

Even so, Pasternak was recognized as one of the outstanding poets of the age; he was still someone to be reckoned with. Until 1958 he escaped the persecution which has been the lot of so many Russian writers of our century, and in 1934 he was even consulted by Stalin about the poetic gifts of Mandelstam (who had just been arrested for composing a satirical poem about the dictator). If he enjoyed a certain immunity at this time, it was not for lack of courage. He did his best to use his position, interceding on behalf of people who had been arrested, and helping those who were in need and prisoners in the labour camps, and feeling a kind of responsibility for the sufferings of others – for instance the deaths of his Georgian friends, the poets Paolo Yashvili and Titsian Tabidze in 1937, and the suicide of Marina Tsvetaeva in 1941. At the time of the monstrous show trials he ran considerable risks by refusing to sign petitions and open letters against the defendants, and on one such occasion, when his signature had been put on a document without his knowledge, he was only dissuaded from creating a scandal by the entreaties of his wife, who was expecting a child. At the beginning of 1938 Zinaida Pasternak gave birth to his second son, Leonid.

The later part of the 1930s was thus a hard time for Pasternak and a time when he found it very difficult to write. During this period he was attempting unsuccessfully to write the novel which

later became *Doctor Zhivago*, but after *Second Birth* he wrote
almost no poetry for ten years. He began, however, to work
seriously as a translator, partly no doubt because this was the way
he could best express himself. He was to become one of the great
verse translators of our time. In 1931, on his first visit to Georgia,
he had begun to translate Georgian poetry, and his versions can
be said to have created this poetry in Russian. Such work was very
successful and well paid, and in 1936 he was able to buy a house
in the writers' settlement of Peredelkino, a village just outside
Moscow which was to be his principal home for the rest of his
life (he also had a small flat in the city). In 1938 he began translating
Shakespeare. The first play he attempted was *Hamlet*, which he
began at the request of Meyerhold; after Meyerhold's arrest in 1939,
it was commissioned by the Moscow Arts Theatre and was
published shortly before the outbreak of war in 1941. His work
on this translation helped him to come through a severe crisis, and
in the winter of 1940–41, after a break of nearly six years, he began
writing his own poetry again. The cycle entitled 'Peredelkino', later
published in the volume *On Early Trains* (1944), brought him great
happiness, because in it he had overcome the dead language of
convention and created a new, simple style (see 'Pine Trees', 'False
Alarm', 'Spring Again').

In June 1941, Hitler's troops marched into Russia. In spite of
hardship and danger, the war of resistance against the German
invader, in which the Russians were fighting side by side with
peoples for whom they had long felt sympathy, was experienced
as a time of common effort in a just cause and as a partial liberation
from the burden of the 'dead letter'. The common aspiration to
victory united people who believed that it would bring back a freer
and more natural way of life. These hopes were to be tragically
disappointed, as Pasternak explained in 1956:

The difficult and tragic war period was the most living period, it was
a time when I experienced the free and joyful return to a feeling of
community with my fellow-countrymen. But when after the magnanimity
of fate, which was manifested in the fact of victory – even a victory bought

at so high a price – when after such generosity on the part of history we returned to the cruelty and sophistry of the darkest and dullest pre-war years, I experienced for the second time [the first being 1936] a feeling of shocked revulsion for the established order, and this time even more strongly and categorically than the first time.

For part of the war period Pasternak was evacuated to Chistopol, five hundred miles east of Moscow, and in 1943 he visited the front line with other authors. During all this time he worked hard and enthusiastically, writing a play about military life (subsequently destroyed), a group of poems on war subjects (see 'Winter Approaches', 'The Old Park', 'Fresco Come to Life'), and translations of *Romeo and Juliet*, *Antony and Cleopatra*, *Othello*, both parts of *Henry IV*, and a volume of poems by the Polish poet Słowacki. His accounts of visits to the front line give a vivid impression of the efforts of the liberated populations to get life going again amid the ashes of towns and villages.

At the same time, in articles on artistic subjects, he stressed the constancy of his aesthetic credo, which he summed up in the concept of subjective-biographical realism. It was the fidelity of the artist's representation of what he has seen or experienced that was for Pasternak the essential element in the art of different schools and periods; he found it in Shakespeare, Tolstoy, Verlaine and Blok, in the French Impressionists, and in the music of Chopin. Of the late nineteenth-century artists he wrote:

> They painted in dabs and spots and half-tones not just because they felt like it or because they were Symbolists. It was reality that was the Symbolist, all flux and fermentation, signifying rather than composing, acting as a symptom or a sign rather than providing satisfaction.

In the aftermath of victory Pasternak felt once again the urge to write a large prose work, a work both rich and popular, which would contain his abiding thoughts about life, the beauty which gives light to everyday existence, art and biography, Pushkin, Tolstoy, and the Bible. He was spurred on partly by the post-war hopes of which he writes on the last page of *Doctor Zhivago*, partly by the awareness that he still had a great deal to say to his contemporaries and that they wanted to listen to him. During the war he had received letters from the front line which had shown him that his voice was heard by far-off unknown people, and in poetry readings in Moscow the audience would prompt him if he forgot a line from a poem. He did not want to lose this contact with the mass of enthusiastic readers and he wanted to be able to tell them what seemed to him to matter most. As a result, he was led to cut himself off more and more from official literary life and to concentrate on the novel that was to become *Doctor Zhivago*.

Against the background of renewed oppression, this choice was experienced by Pasternak as a return to a former freedom and independence, a return to old values, and a return to the Christian religion, which is so important in the novel. It was a dangerous choice and he was well aware that it could have dire consequences for him. At the time when he began to work on his novel, he wrote the poem 'Hamlet', in which one can hear the Gethsemane note of the solitary, predestined sacrificial act. And indeed the circumstances were not propitious. A new ideological pogrom began in 1946, and many of Pasternak's friends and acquaintances were arrested. The terror continued and increased throughout the period when he was working on *Doctor Zhivago*. He lived with the knowledge that his turn might come at any time, and in one letter he wrote: 'Of course I am prepared for anything. Why should it happen to everyone else and not to me?'

There were other sorrows and difficulties at this time. He was deeply grieved by his father's death in 1945, and the growing number of deaths among the friends of his youth reminded him of his own age. For his wife, the greatest tragedy was the death of her eldest son, Adrian, after five years of suffering. As she herself said, this loss burned her up, leaving her a stern, worried, and joyless woman. At about the same time another woman entered Pasternak's life. In 1946 he met and fell in love with Olga Ivinskaya; she was some twenty-two years his junior and was working in the offices of the literary journal, *Novy Mir*. It was she who inspired many of the later love poems, and she was in many ways the prototype for Lara in *Doctor Zhivago*. In 1949 she was sent to a forced labour camp where she remained until Stalin's death in 1953; thereafter, she was close to Pasternak until the time of his death.

In the post-war period, money was constantly in short supply. Apart from the considerable expenses of his house and family, Pasternak sent sums of money every month to various needy people. Neither his prose nor his poetry was published after 1945, and as a result he had to take on major new translations every year. These included *King Lear* and *Macbeth*, both parts of Goethe's *Faust*, Schiller's *Maria Stuart*, the complete poetic works of the Georgian poet N. Baratashvili and the Hungarian S. Petöfi. At every new edition of his translations, zealous editors pursued him with demands for alterations to bring them closer to the original. *Hamlet* was reworked twelve times in all, and Pasternak once said jokingly that he had got utterly confused and that if he had the time and no editor it would be worth starting again from scratch and translating it freely. All this took up a vast amount of his time – 'but I shall still write my novel in the twenty-fifth hour of the day', he said.

Three parts were written in less than a year, and in the autumn of 1948 four parts, which originally made up the first book, already existed in typescript. Pasternak let people see his work quite freely and sent it by post to various towns, where it was avidly read. The text of the novel kept growing. In 1950 came the fifth and sixth parts, and in the autumn of 1952, while finishing his translation of *Faust*, Pasternak was completing the chapters about the partisans. In the same year he had a severe heart attack, which brought him close to death. He was not frightened but accepted the pain and danger with a feeling of liberation and happiness, which came from the knowledge of what he had done and the certainty that his family was provided for, at least in the short term. Three months after his illness he wrote:

In that moment, which seemed like my last, I wanted more than ever to talk with God, to praise all things visible, capture them and record them. 'Dear Lord', I whispered, 'I thank you for applying the paint so richly and that in your creation of life and death you speak to us in splendour and music, I thank you that you have made me an artist, that creativity is your school, and that all my life you have been preparing me for this night.' And I exulted and wept for joy.

These are the sentiments which permeate such late poems as 'When the Weather Clears'.

Similarly, the novel about Yury Zhivago and the poems attributed to him are an expression of this joy that conquers the fear of death. In 1955 Pasternak wrote:

My life in recent years has been so full, so clear, so absorbed in the work I love, that it has been an almost continuous festival of the soul for me. I am more than contented, I am happy with it, and the novel is an outlet and an expression for this happiness.

His own experience led him to write that immortality is another, somewhat stronger name for life, and he considered this thought to be the basis of his understanding of Christian history. In Part 1 of the novel, Nikolay Vedenyapin says:

'The centuries and generations began to breathe freely only after the coming of Christ. Only then did the life through posterity begin, and as a result human beings no longer die in the ditch, but at home in history, in the midst of labours devoted to the overcoming of death.'

One of Pasternak's principal aims in *Doctor Zhivago* was to communicate to his contemporaries that awareness of the organic warmth and colour of life which had been connected from of old with the gospels. But by the late 1950s Russian society had changed so completely, that, as he put it, even the language had disappeared which was spoken at the turn of the century. He had therefore to find a new way of expressing time-honoured thoughts and attitudes, and to this end adopted a plainer and more ordinary language than that of his youthful writing, and repudiated his earlier manner, which he saw as being too affected or obscure. His remark 'I do not like my pre-1940 style' is typical of his self-criticism, and has led many readers to believe that there are two poets in Pasternak, the young innovator and the wiser and simpler author of the later poems. There is certainly a difference of style between *My Sister Life* and the Zhivago poems, and this may sometimes mask the continuity of themes and values. At the same time, many of Pasternak's most important qualities can be seen in both his early and late work – above all his feelings for the movement and constant renewal of life and for the richness of the world. Like many writers who have made similar statements, he had his own good reasons for turning away from his earlier writing, but readers remain free to see the value of both.

Each of the twenty-five poems written between 1946 and 1953 and attributed to Yury Zhivago quickly became known in manuscript. About half of them were published in the journal *Znamya* (*Banner*) in the spring of 1954, but the rest – for the most part poems with overtly Christian themes – were not published in Russia during Pasternak's lifetime, and have still not been published. Even so, thousands of people know them by heart.

In 1956 work began in the State Publishing House on a selection of Pasternak's poetry, for which he again revised his early poems and wrote new ones. His *Essay in Autobiography* was intended as an introduction to this volume. There were also plans to publish *Doctor Zhivago*, but it was rejected by the journal *Novy Mir* and delay followed delay. Meanwhile a representative of the Italian Communist Party was given a copy of the novel and took it to Italy. In November 1957 it was published in Russian by Feltrinelli of Milan. Then, in October 1958, Pasternak was awarded the Nobel Prize for literature; this was taken as a recognition of the value and importance of *Doctor Zhivago*, and it immediately started an official witchhunt against him in the Soviet Union. He was threatened at the very least with expulsion from the country, but thanks to the intervention of Pandit Nehru, this threat was averted. At the same time, fearing for those close to him, he was driven to sign printed statements which he had not written.

Pasternak was not sent into exile or arrested, but all publication of his translations came to a halt and he was deprived of his livelihood. In a letter of this time (see also 'Nobel Prize'), he writes that he feels as if he were living on the moon or in a fourth dimension. He was world-famous, yet his name was anathema in his native land; he was poor and uncertain of being able to support his dependents, yet he received hundreds of letters with requests for help from his income abroad – letters in response to which he gladly sent instructions to his foreign publishers. He also received many impossible proposals and invitations from abroad to give poetry readings, to lecture, to travel, and to speak at conferences. From leading literary figures of Europe and America – Camus, Faulkner, Hemingway, T. S. Eliot, René Char, Stephen Spender, and John Steinbeck – came direct or indirect expressions of support and sympathy. Sometimes there were no letters for weeks, then he would get fifty in one day.

The strain of all this did not disturb the rhythm of work which Pasternak used all his strength to keep going. He had accumulated new poems for the selection which never appeared, and they make up his last complete book, *When the Weather Clears*. In January 1959 he wrote the final poem in this book and gave the whole collection an epigraph from Proust: 'A book is a great cemetery in which you can no longer read the obliterated names on most of the gravestones.'

In the summer of 1959 he began *The Blind Beauty*, a play about an enslaved artist during the period of serfdom in Russia. A great deal of his time was taken up with his world-wide correspondence, since he did not want to leave unacknowledged any expressions of concern or sympathy. At the beginning of 1960, while fighting against a gradually increasing pain in his back, he copied out the first scenes of the play. Slowly he became aware that the pain was the sign of a fatal illness, lung cancer. His condition got worse in April, and he was forced to take to his bed, leaving his work unfinished. For a month and a half he endured great suffering courageously and without losing consciousness, attempting all the time to console his family and friends and the doctors and nurses who were looking after him. He died on the evening of 30 May.

The authorities did their best to play down his death; only a small notice appeared in the *Literary Gazette*. But in spite of official silence and disapproval, many thousands of people travelled out from Moscow to his funeral in the village of Peredelkino where he had lived. Volunteers carried his open coffin to his burial place and those who were present recited from memory the banned poem 'Hamlet'. Since that day his beautiful grave has been a place of pilgrimage.

Boris Pasternak

SELECTED
POEMS

BEGINNINGS

I T's February. Weeping, take ink.
   Find words in a sobbing rush
For February, while black spring
Burns through the rumbling slush.

And take a cab. Ride for a rouble
Through wheel racket and bells' throbbing
To where the downpour makes more din
Than the sound of ink and sobbing;

Where rooks in thousands, like charred pears
Windfallen from their branching skies,
Drop into puddles and bring down
Desolation into deep eyes.

Thawed patches underneath show black,
The wind is furrowed with cries, and then,
The more suddenly the more surely,
Verses sob from the pen.

                                    1912

T HE sleepy garden scatters beetles
   Like bronze cinders from braziers.
Level with me and with my candle
There hangs a flowering universe.

As if into a new religion
I cross the threshold of this night,
Where the grey decaying poplar
Has veiled the moon's bright edge from sight,

Where the orchard surf whispers of apples,
Where the pond is an opened secret,
Where the garden hangs, as if on piles,
And holds the sky in front of it.

1913

VENICE

THE clatter of a cloudy pane
   Awoke me in the small hours.
It hung in a gondola rank
And vacancy weighed on the oars.

The trident of hushed guitars
Was hanging like Scorpio's stars
Above a marine horizon
Untouched by the smoking sun.

In the domain of the zodiac
The chord was a lonely sound.
Untroubled below by the trident,
The port moved its mists around.

At some time the earth had split off,
Capsized palaces gone to wrack.
A fortress loomed up like a planet;
Like a planet, houses spun back.

And the secret of life without root
I understood as the day surfaced:
My dreams and my eyes had more room
To grope on their own through the mist.

And like the foam of mad blossom
And like the foam of rabid lips,
Among glimmering shadows broke loose
The chord that knew no fingertips.

1914

OVER THE BARRIERS

WINTER SKY

Out of the smoky air now are plucked down
  Stars for the past week frozen in flight.
Head over heels reels the skaters' club,
Clinking its rink with the glass of the night.

Slower, slower, skater, step slow-er,
Cutting the curve as you swerve by.
Every turn a constellation
Scraped by the skate into Norway's sky.

Fetters. of frozen iron shackle the air.
Hey, skaters! There it's all the same
That night is on earth with its ivory eyes
Snake-patterned like a domino game;

That the moon, like a numb retriever's tongue,
Is freezing to bars as tight as a vice;
That mouths, like forgers' mouths, are filled
Brim-full with lava of breathtaking ice.

                                    1914–1916

THE URALS FOR THE FIRST TIME

Without obstetrician, in darkness, unconscious,
  The towering Urals, hands clawing the night,
Yelled out in travail and fainting away,
Blinded by agony, gave birth to light.

In thunder, the masses and bronzes of mountains,
Accidentally struck, avalanched down.
The train went on panting. And somewhere this made
The spectres of firs go shyly to ground.

The smoke-haze at dawn was a soporific,
Administered slyly – to mountain and factory –
By men lighting stoves, by sulphurous dragons,
As thieves slip a drug in a traveller's tea.

They came to in fire. From the crimson horizon
Down to their timberline destination,
Asians were skiing with crowns for the pines
And summoning them to their coronation.

And the pines, shaggy monarchs, in order of precedence
Rising up, stepped out, row on row
On to a damascened cloth-of-gold carpet
Spread with the orange of crusted snow.

1916

SPRING

How many sticky buds, how many candle-ends
Are glued to the branches now! April
Is lit. The wind from the park reeks of puberty
And the woods are more blatant still.

A tight loop of feathered throats holds the wood's windpipe
Lassoed like a steer, and it groans
In nets as the gladiatorial organ
Steel-throated sonatas intones.

Now, Poetry, be a Greek sponge with suckers
And let the green succulence drench
You, under the trees on the sodden wood
Of a green-mottled garden bench.

Grow sumptuous flounces and furbelows,
Suck clouds and gullies in hour by hour,
And, Poetry, tonight I'll squeeze you out
To make the thirsty paper flower.

1916

SWIFTS

At twilight the swifts have no way
    Of stemming the cool blue cascade.
It bursts from clamouring throats,
A torrent that cannot be stayed.

At twilight the swifts have no way
Of holding back, high overhead,
Their clarion shouting: Oh, triumph,
Look, look, how the earth has fled!

As steam billows up from a kettle,
The furious stream hisses by –
Look, look – there's no room for the earth
Between the ravine and the sky.

1914–1916

IMPROVISATION

I was feeding the flock of keys out of my hand
To a beating of wings. I was standing on tiptoe,
My hands reaching out to the splashing and screaming.
My sleeve was rolled up and night brushed my elbow.

And it was pitch dark. And there was a pond
And waves. And the love-birds and suchlike, it seemed,
Would surely be pecked to death long before those
Whose black, strident, savage beaks screamed.

And there was a pond. And it was pitch dark
Except where the lilies like torches were flickering.
A wave was gnawing the planks of the dinghy.
And birds at my elbow were snapping and bickering.

Night rattled like phlegm in the throats of the ponds.
The fledgling had yet to be fed, it seemed,
And the females would peck it to death long before
The roulades would cease in the gullet that screamed.

1916

MARBURG

I quivered. I flared up, and then was extinguished.
I shook. I had made a proposal – but late,
Too late. I was scared, and she had refused me.
I pity her tears, am more blessed than a saint.

I stepped into the square. I could be counted
Among the twice-born. Every leaf on the lime,
Every brick was alive, caring nothing for me,
And reared up to take leave for the last time.

The paving-stones glowed and the street's brow was swarthy.
From under their lids the cobbles looked grim,
Scowled up at the sky, and the wind like a boatman
Was rowing through limes. And each was an emblem.

Be that as it may, I avoided their glances,
Averted my gaze from their greeting or scowling.
I wanted no news of their getting and spending.
I had to get out, so as not to start howling.

The tiles were afloat, and an unblinking noon
Regarded the rooftops. And someone, somewhere
In Marburg, was whistling, at work on a crossbow,
And someone else dressing for the Trinity fair.

Devouring the clouds, the sand showed yellow,
A storm wind was rocking the bushes to and fro,
And the sky had congealed where it touched a sprig
Of woundwort that staunched its flow.

Like any rep Romeo hugging his tragedy,
I reeled through the city rehearsing you.
I carried you all that day, knew you by heart
From the comb in your hair to the foot in your shoe.

And when in your room I fell to my knees,
Embracing this mist, this perfection of frost
(How lovely you are!), this smothering turbulence,
What were you thinking? 'Be sensible!' Lost!

Here lived Martin Luther. The Brothers Grimm, there.
And all things remember and reach out to them:
The sharp-taloned roofs. The gravestones. The trees.
And each is alive. And each is an emblem.

I shall not go tomorrow. Refusal –
More final than parting. We're quits. All is clear.
And if I abandon the streetlamps, the banks –
Old pavingstones, what will become of me here?

The mist on all sides will unpack its bags,
In both windows will hang up a moon.
And melancholy will slide over the books
And settle with one on the ottoman.

Then why am I scared? Insomnia I know
Like grammar, by heart. I have grown used to that.
In line with the four square panes of my window
Dawn will lay out her diaphanous mat.

The nights now sit down to play chess with me
Where ivory moonlight chequers the floor.
It smells of acacia, the windows are open,
And passion, a grey witness, stands by the door.

The poplar is king. I play with insomnia.
The queen is a nightingale I can hear calling.
I reach for the nightingale. And the night wins.
The pieces make way for the white face of morning.

1915–1956

58

MY SISTER LIFE

About These Poems

On pavements I shall trample them
  With broken glass and sun in turn.
In winter I shall open them
For the peeling ceiling to learn.

The garret will start to declaim
With a bow to the window-frame.
Calamities, eccentricities
Will leapfrog to the cornices.

The blizzard will not month after month
Scour ends and beginnings with snow.
I shall remember: there is the sun.
And see: the light changed long ago.

When Christmas with a jackdaw glint
Peeps out, the day will suddenly
Brighten, revealing many things
Unnoticed by my love and me.

Shielding my face at the window
And scarfed against the rasping air,
I shall shout to the kids: Hey, you,
What century is it out there?

Who beat a pathway to the door,
To the entrance walled up with snow,
While I was smoking with Byron
And drinking with Edgar Poe?

Received in Darial as a friend,
As in the armoury or hell,
I dipped my life, like Lermontov's
Passion, like lips in alcohol.

1917

M Y sister, Life, is today overflowing
  And smashing herself in spring rain on our coats,
But people with monocles are not amused
And bite, quite politely, like snakes in the oats.

The older ones have their own reasons for this.
But yours is a comical reason, no doubt:
That under the storm, eyes and lawns appear lilac
And mignonette sweetens the wind from the south.

That when, on your journey in May, you're consulting
The timetable on the Kamyshin line,
The Bible itself is not more exalting.
Your eyes, mesmerized, are to all else blind.

That, setting, the sun has only to highlight
Girls crowding the railway track, as the train slows,
For me to discover it is not my station,
The sun to extend its regrets as it goes.

And splashing a third time, the bell swims behind,
Its 'Sorry, not here' sounding near, further, far.
The burning night filters in under the blind
And the steppe plunges on from the steps to the star;

Winking and blinking, but sweetly somewhere,
My love, like a mirage, and others all sleep
While, splashing along carriage footboards, the heart
Scatters bright windows across the dark steppe.

1917

THE WEEPING GARDEN

IT's terrible: dripping and listening
If it's as much alone as ever –
Crumpling a lacy branch at the window –
Or if there's an eavesdropper.

But audibly the porous earth
Is choking with so much growth
And in the distance, as in August,
Midnight ripens with the harvest.

No sound. And no one hiding.
Having made sure it's on its own
It returns to its old game – sliding
From gable to gutter and down.

I'll raise it to my lips and listen
If I'm as much alone as ever –
Ready to sob if I have to –
Or if there's an eavesdropper.

But all is quiet. Not a leaf stirs.
Nothing anywhere to be seen,
Except the gulps and splashing galoshes
And sighs and tears in between.

1917

MIRROR

IN the mirror is steaming a cocoa cup,
  A lace curtain sways, and along
The path to the chaos of garden and steppe
The mirror runs to the swing.

There swaying pines needle the air with resin;
There, fussily bending to look
For its glasses, the garden is combing the grass;
There Shade is reading a book.

And into the background, the darkness, beyond
The gate into grasslands sweet
With drugs, down the path, between snail-trails and twigs
The quartz shimmers white in the heat.

The soul can't be mined, like a seam with saltpetre,
Or hacked out, like gems, with a pick.
The huge garden shakes in the hall, in the mirror –
But the glass does not break.

I cannot extinguish the light of my eyes
In this hypnotic domain,
As slugs in the garden will plug the eyes
Of statues after rain.

Water tickles the ear, and a siskin,
Chirping, hurdles the sticks.
You can stain their lips with bilberry juice,
You will not put an end to their tricks.

The garden raises its fist to the mirror;
The room and the garden shake.
It runs to the swing, and catches it, shakes it,
And still the glass does not break.

1917

Rain

She's here with me. Come strum, pour, laugh,
  Tear the twilight through and through!
Drown, flow down, an epigraph
To a love like you!

Scurry like a silk-worm
And beat the window's drum.
Combine, entwine,
And let the darkness come!

Noon midnight, cloudburst – come for her!
Walking home, soaked to the skin!
Whole tree-loads of water
On eyes, cheeks, jasmin!

Hosanna to Egyptian darkness!
Drops chuckle, slide, collide,
And suddenly the air smells new
As to patients who've come through.

Let's run and pluck – as from guitars
Guitarists pluck a phrase –
The garden Saint-Gothard
Washed with a lime-tree haze.

1917

FROM SUPERSTITION

A matchbox with an orange
⠀⠀Is my little room.
Not squalid hotel cells
Till the morgue, till the tomb!

A second time, from superstition,
Here I unpack my things.
The wallpaper is the colour of oak
And the door sings.

My hand would be still on the latch
And you evading me yet,
And forelock and fringe would touch
And lip touch violet.

Dear heart, for old times' sake, your dress
Now swaying to and fro,
Like a snowdrop greeting April,
Is whispering 'Hello'.

Perish the thought that you are no vestal:
In with a chair you came,
And took down my life from the shelf
And blew the dust from the name.

⠀⠀⠀⠀⠀⠀⠀⠀⠀⠀1917

Oars Crossed

Sleepy the lake's breast, the boat beats in it,
  Willows stoop down, lips kissing collarbone,
Elbow and rowlock – oh, wait a minute,
This sort of thing can happen to anyone!

This is just ... this is all trivial ...
This just means – with hesitant fingertips
Ruffling the petals of the white camomile,
Touching the lilac's pale flesh with your lips.

This just means – embracing the firmament,
Hugging great Hercules; this just means
For centuries, centuries on end,
Squandering your substance on nightingales!

                                        1917

Spring Rain

It grinned to the bird-cherry, sobbed, and soaked
  The gloss of carriages, the flutter of pines.
Under the bulging moon, fiddlers in single file
Make their way to the theatre. Citizens, form lines!

Puddles on stone. Like a throat full of tears,
Deep in the heart of a rose's furnace
Damp diamonds burn, and on them, on clouds,
On eyelids, the wet lash of happiness.

The moon for the first time models in plaster
Epic queues, tossing dresses, the power
Of enraptured lips; it models a bust
Modelled by no one until this hour.

Whose is the heart in which all this blood
Rushed from the cheeks, rushed in a flood
To glory? The minister's fingertips
Have squeezed together aortas and lips.

Not the night, not the rain, not the chorus
Shouting 'Hurrah, Kerensky!' but now
The blinding emergence into the forum
From catacombs thought to have no way out.

Not roses, not mouths, not the roar
Of crowds, but here, in the forum, is felt
The surf of Europe's wavering night,
Proud of itself on our asphalt.

1917

MALADIES OF THE EARTH

L ET only laughter resound! Oh, more!
   Mother of pearl, a Niagara swarm
Of staphylococci, a drenching roar,
And incisors flash in the storm.

Stop – that's enough! Unwavering titans
Will choke in the dark vaults of noon.
Tetanus, trembling, will gather shadows,
Dust paralyse grass-snakes soon.

And here's the rain! Hydrophobia
Flashes, whirls, drops of saliva shine.
But from where? From cloud, field, Klyazma,
Or from the sardonic pine?

Whose verses have made such a din
As dumbfounds even the thunder's wrath?
You have to be raving mad
To agree to be the earth.

1917

DEFINITION OF CREATIVITY

RIPPING a shirtfront open,
Shaggy as Beethoven's bared chest,
Its hand overshadows, like chessmen,
Night and passion, conscience and rest,

And is making – under the sway
Of some tumultuous sorrow –
A black king ready for doomsday,
Dark horseman with pawns in its shadow.

But the garden, whose chilled stars exhale
Fragrance straight from the cellar,
Is filled as by a nightingale
With Tristan's brimming song for Isolde.

And the gardens, and fences, and ponds,
And the galaxies howling at large
Are only the currents of passion
That human hearts discharge.

1917

SPARROW HILLS

Put your breast under kisses, as under a tap!
For summer will not always bubble up,
And we cannot pump out the accordion's roar
Night after night round the dusty floor.

I've heard tell of old age. Terrible prophecies!
No breaker will throw up its hands to the stars.
They say things you can't believe. No face in the grass,
No heart in the ponds, no God in the trees.

Stir up your soul then! Make it all foam today.
Where are your eyes? This is the world's high noon.
Up there, thoughts cluster in a fleecy spray
Of cloud, heat, and woodpeckers, pine-needle and cone.

At this point the tramlines of town break off.
Beyond, the pines serve. Beyond, rails cannot pass.
Beyond, it is Sunday. Breaking off branches,
The glade runs for cover, slipping on grass.

Scattering noons and Trinity and country walks –
The world is always like this, the wood believes.
So the thicket devised it, so the clearing was told,
So it pours from the clouds – on us in our shirt-sleeves.

1917

STEPPE

How good it was then to go out into quietness!
  The steppe's boundless seascape flows to the sky.
The feather grass sighs, ants rustle in it,
And the keening mosquito floats by.

Haystacks have lined themselves up with clouds,
The cones of volcanoes cooling to grey.
The boundless steppe has grown silent and damp;
It rocks you, buffets you, bears you away.

Mist has surrounded us here like the sea,
Burs clutching our stockings, and how good today
To wander the steppe like the shore of the sea;
It rocks you, buffets you, bears you away.

Is that not a haystack? Who knows?
Is that not our rick coming closer? Yes. Found!
The very one. Rick, mist, and steppe,
Rick, mist, and steppe all round.

Off to the right runs the Milky Way
To Kerch, like a highroad the cattle pound
To dust. It will take your breath away
Behind the huts: such distances all round.

The mist soporific, the grass like honey,
The Milky Way in feather grass drowned.
The mist will disperse and the night will embrace
The haystack and steppe all round.

Crepuscular midnight stands by the road,
Where the stars have spilled from its purse.
You cannot go over the road past the fence
Without trampling the universe.

When did the stars ever grow so low
And midnight fall to the feather-grassed ground
And muslin mist catch alight and cling,
Thirst for the grand finale to sound?

Let the steppe judge between us and night decide
When and when not: in the Beginning
Did Ants Creep on Grass, did Mosquitoes Keen,
Did Bur Clutch at Stocking?

Shut your eyes, darling, or you will be blinded!
The steppe is tonight as before the Fall:
All lapped in peace, all like a parachute,
A rearing vision, all.

1917

STORM, INSTANTANEOUS FOREVER

THEN summer took leave of the platform
    And waiting room. Raising his cap,
The storm at night for souvenir
Took snap after dazzling snap.

The lilac darkened. And the storm
Came bounding in from the meadows
With a sheaf of lightning flashes
To light the office windows.

And when malicious delight ran
Down corrugated iron in torrents,
And like charcoal on a drawing
The downpour crashed against the fence,

The avalanche of consciousness began
To glimmer: light, it seemed, would soon
Flood even those corners of reason
Where now it is bright as noon.

1917

My friend, you ask who gives the order
For the holy fool's speech to burn?

L ET words drop, as resin
    And orange peel casually
Rain down in a garden
Lightly, lightly, lightly.

No need to inquire
Why so ceremonially
Rose-madder and lemon
Stipple trees annually.

Or who hung the thorns
With tears, and sluiced book-lined
Shelves and a music stand
Through the grille of a slatted blind;

Who paints the little rug
Behind the door with rowan,
With exquisite italic
Like trembling hessian.

You ask me who instructs
August to be imperial,
Who counts nothing trivial,
Who patiently perfects

The leaf of the maple,
And since the days of Ecclesiastes
Has remained at his post
Hewing alabaster?

You ask who gives the order
That the lips of the aster
And dahlia shall suffer?
That broom leaves shall flutter
From grey caryatids
Down to damp flagstones
Of autumn hospitals?

You ask who gives the order?
The omnipotent god of details,
The omnipotent god of love,
Of Jagiello and Jadwiga.

It may be that our knowledge
At the graveside fails.
But life, like autumn stillness,
Is composed of details.

1917

THEMES AND VARIATIONS

From THEME AND VARIATIONS

You did not see them,
The living sculptures of ancient Egypt,
With quiet eyes, motionless and dumb,
With brows shining from imperial coronation.

*

But you did not see them, did not perceive
Between us and those sphinxes the mysterious bond.

APOLLYON GRIGORYEV

THEME

A cliff and gale. A cliff and cloak and hat.
A cliff and ... Pushkin. The man who even now,
With eyes shut, stands and sees in the Sphinx
Not the mad things we see; not the guesses
Of baffled Oedipus, not a riddle,
But a forbear: the flat-lipped Hamite
Who has endured the sands like smallpox,
Is pockmarked by the Sahara,
And nothing else. A cliff and gale.

Beer raving, cascading off
The moustache of precipice, headland, cliff,
Spit, shoal, and knot. The blazing and roar
Of the deep, drenched with moonlight
As from a washtub. Sucking gale and fume
And thunder. Light, as day. All lit by foam.
You can't tear your eyes from that sight.
Surf pounding the Sphinx spares no candles
And fresh ones it promptly rekindles.
A cliff and gale. A cliff and cloak and hat.
The Sphinx's lips inhale the salty breath
Of fogs. The sand all round is smeared
With medusan kisses of death.

He does not know the mermaids' scales.
And can a man believe in their fishtails
Who once has drunk from their knee cups
The gleam of stars, pulsing on ice?

A cliff and storm and, hidden from all
Indiscreet eyes, strangest, most mild,
Playing since the age of Psammetichus
Across the desert's cheekbones, the laughter of a child . . .

VARIATION 3

S TA R S were racing. Headlands washed themselves.
  Salt was growing blind. And tears were drying.
Bedrooms lay in darkness. Thoughts were racing,
And the Spinx heard the desert sighing.

Candles swam. The colossus's blood
Seemed to be cooling. Lips grew fuller
With the desert's slow blue smile.
At the tide's ebb, night lost colour.

Waves were touched by a breeze from Morocco.
Simoon! Archangel snored in its snows.
Candles swam. The draft of the 'Prophet'
Was drying, and day on the Ganges rose.

1918

SPRING

S PRING, I come in from the street, where the poplar is shaken,
  Where distance is frightened, the house afraid it will fall,
Where the air is blue as the laundry bag
Of a patient released from hospital.

Where evening is empty, an unfinished tale
Left in the air by a star with no sequel,
Bewildering thousands of noisy eyes,
Expressionless, unfathomable.

1918

JANUARY 1919

THAT year! How often at the window
'Throw yourself out', the old year would say.
But this, with its *Christmas Carol*,
Has driven all that way.

It whispers, 'Forget it. Shake yourself',
Its mercury stretching at the sun's smile,
Where last year poured out strychnine
And sank in the cyanide phial.

Its morning, its outstretched hand,
Its hair blowing lazily to and fro,
Draw peace up past the window-sill
For gable, philosopher, crow.

See, it stretches in a ray of light
After shifting snow from the ground.
Audacious and excited,
It bellows for drink, throws its weight around.

It's out of its mind, and nothing
Can stop that clatter in the yard below.
There's not a sorrow in all the world
That cannot be cured with snow.

1919

Thus they begin. At two they rush
From nurse into thickets of melody,
They chirp, they whistle, and words
Appear by the age of three.

Thus they begin to understand.
And in the starting turbine's din
It seems as if mother is not mother,
You are not you, and home is foreign.

What can the fearful beauty do,
The lilac on the park-bench here,
Except steal children from their homes?
Thus suspicions appear.

Thus fears ripen. How can he let
A star beyond his arm's reach spin,
When he is Faust, a visionary?
Thus Romanies begin.

Thus seas reveal themselves, afloat
Above fences, where windows should shine,
And waves lift sudden as a sigh.
Thus iambs fall into line.

Thus summer nights, falling face down
In oat-fields, pray: Thy will be done.
Rebuke the dawn with your iris.
Thus they challenge the rising sun.

Thus they begin to live by verse.

1919

S LANTING pictures, streaming in
  From the candle-snuffing street,
I cannot teach not to fly off
Their hooks and fall on to rhyming feet.

What if the Universe wears a mask?
What if no latitudes exist
With lips they would not seal with putty
Against the winter's blast?

But things tear off their masks,
Lose honour, lose control,
When they have reason to sing,
When rain has occasion to fall.

1922

NINETEEN HUNDRED AND FIVE

MUTINY AT SEA

EVERYTHING palls.
   You alone will never grow stale.
Day after day
Goes past and years go past
And thousands and thousands of years
In the waves' white energy
Hiding
In the white spice of acacias
Perhaps you,
Sea,
Will grind them and wash them away.

You recline on piled nets,
You burble,
Spring-like, playing the fool,
And like a curl at the ear
The current just tickles the stern.
You are visiting children.
But with what an unparalleled storm
You make your reply
When distance insists you return.

Antediluvian space
Rages with foam and grows hoarse.
Regular surf
Goes insane
From the masses of work.
Everything flies apart
And howls and expires as it will
And hog-like with slime
Against the piles goes berserk.

The limpness of sails
Is driven hard back
By the sameness
Of colours gone mad,
And closer the wall of the downpour comes,
And lower still sinks the sky
And hangs at a slant,
Flies head over heels,
And plumbs the depths with its gulls.

Through the galvanic gloom
Of turbulent clouds
Awkwardly
Waddling, crawling,
Ships make their way to port.
Lightning, blue-legged,
Hops like frogs in a puddle.
Lanky rigging,
Mainstay and shrouds,
Flogs back and forth.

It was time for a snooze.
Crabs clambered about,
And under the core
Of the sinking sun
Burdock heads bowed.
A verst and a half from Tendr,
Against the battleship's steaming
Crest, the sea was purring,
Shot with orange,
Gleaming.

The sun set.
And suddenly
Electricity blazed through *Potemkin*.

From spar-deck to galley
A scum of flies tumbled about.
The meat was high ...
And darkness came down on the sea.
Light grumbled till morning
And at glimmering daybreak went out.

Slivers
Of morning ripple
Flickered
Like quicksilver razors,
Along the silhouette's base,
And towering over them
The battleship started to breathe
And came to consciousness.
They chanted a prayer,
Started to swab the deck,
And set gunnery targets in place.

At dinner they gave the borsch a wide berth;
Were silently eating
Black bread and water
When suddenly came the cry:
'All on deck!
And fall in
In two watches!'
A uniformed somebody,
Face dark with fury,
Bawled out:
'Atten-*shun*!'
Seven hundred harangued
From the anchor locker by one.

'Any complaints?
There's borsch, if you want to eat!
If you don't, there's the yard-arm!
Dismiss!'
They stood, hardly daring to breathe.
Then suddenly, all
In a stumbling rush,
Broke away from the locker
And ran to the guns.
'Halt!
Stay where you are!'
Roared
The frantic apostle of borsch.

A few lagged behind.
He stood in their way.
'What, at it again!'
He gave a command:
'Bosun,
Fetch a tarpaulin!
Marines, keep them there!'
The others
Stood huddled, their backs to the turret,
Awaiting in horror the punishment
Hovering in the air.

They heard their hearts beating,
And one
Who could bear it no longer
Howled:
'Shipmates,
What's this then?'
And running a hand through his hair:

'Let 'em 'av it, the buggers!
Get rifles –
For freedom!'
A clatter of feet and steel
Rolled away
To the scuppers.

And mutiny swept
In a rush
To the top of the mizzen
And leaped
From there
Like a flail
Describing an arc.
'Why set on each other?
I'll get you, you son
Of a bitch!'
Rat-tat-tat . . .
A shot at the target,
A burst on the run.

Rat-tat-tat . . .
And bullets were skipping on decks,
Off decks –
Rat-tat-tat –
At the sea
And the swimmers.
'Is the bugger still there?'
Volleys at water and air.
'Aha,
So you don't like complaints!'
Volleys, volleys,
And feet-first overboard,
Quick march to Port Arthur.

But the stokers were restless,
Not knowing for sure
How things stood up above,
When, shadowy over the boilers,
Over the engine room grating
Strode
Gigantic
Matyushenko,
And into the roaring inferno
He bellowed:
'Steve boy,
We've won!'

The stoker climbed up.
They embraced.
'Let's live without nursemaids.
Don't worry,
They're guarded
And the rest got some lead and a swim.
But I came down to ask
Have we a young engineer?'
'There's a lad . . .'
'That's O.K.
Send him up to me here.'

The day passed.
And at dusk,
Enfurled in a curtain of smoke,
A sailor's voice boomed from the megaphone:
'Up with the anchor!'

The voice in the cloud was still;
The battleship, turning,
Made for Odessa, orange
Against a dark crest,
Burning.

1925–6

POEMS OF
VARIOUS YEARS

PUTTING OUT TO SEA

LISTEN to the rippling drip of salt,
Paddle-wheels rumbling down below.
Taking the harbour by its shoulders,
Past the warehouses we go.

Splash and splash and splash without echo.
Running in every direction,
The birch-bark expanse of moaning sea
Flares up with a pink reflection.

Hiss of burning birch bark
And the crackle of crab shells.
Expanse expanding, and the sea
Shuddering as it swells.

Shore recedes in a dark wood
Of angular, dreary firs.
Idling gloomily, the sea
Looks down on travellers.

Shoreward, searching for berries,
On through the woods, with a crash
Disconcerting the ship's side,
Travels the widening splash.

Visible still, still visible
The shore, and the road's surface
Speckled, though altered already
And, like disaster, limitless.

Swung in a fearsome half circle,
Changing places suddenly,
Masts canter in through the gateway,
The gates of the wide open sea.

Here it is! And as a foretaste
Of raging delights for the sailor,
Sounding the wreck-strewn depths,
A gull dips, like a bailer.

Gulf of Finland, 1922

LILY OF THE VALLEY

HEAT since morning. But push aside
      The bushes, and high noon beyond
Comes crashing down with all its weight,
Exploding into diamond.

It tumbles down in ribs and rays,
And sunbeam facets smoulder
Like a glazier's box
Dumped down from a sweaty shoulder.

Disguising itself with night,
Here whiteness makes up with pitch.
Here spring in all its newness
Is fabulous as Uglich.

Heat's merciless massacre
Stops short of the wood's dark ways.
And now you enter the birch grove,
Encounter each other's gaze.

But you have been forestalled.
Someone below is watching you:
The gully's damp floor is studded
With lily-of-the-valley dew.

Detached, it raises its drops –
Half lifting, half burdened by them,
One finger, two, from the leaf,
One and a half from the stem.

Its ears like clinging kidskin
Rustle but make no sound.
Night's dusky hands lay out
White kid gloves on the ground.

1927

NIGHT VIOLET

NOT long ago along this woodland ride
 The rain paced, like a surveyor. Here,
Lily of the valley is bowed with spoon-bait,
And water hides in the mullein's ear.

Their lobes in a pine-root cradle
Are burdened with dew at dusk.
They dislike the daylight. Each grows by itself
And gives off its own sweet musk.

When people are drinking tea in their dachas,
Mist releases the mosquito fleet,
And night, unexpectedly strumming a tune
On the moon, stands blanched in the wheat,

Then everything smells of night violets:
Summers and faces and thoughts. All events
That can be salvaged from the past
And those the future has still to dispense.

1927

GATHERING STORM

APPROACHING, you advance on foot
Across the fields – and keeping step
Will gain the cliff, fling off your pack,
And roll your thunder down a slope.

Like a cannon-ball cast before
Peter the Great, it will skip through
The meadow and topple a wood-stack,
Slamming its logs askew.

Then melancholy like a bridge
Will seal off the distance and soon
Smell of trenches. Rain. Swallows will swirl,
Poplars parade in a ghostly platoon.

A rumour will go through the heights
That you – before the Swedes – were here,
And a chill from the forward scouts
Will gallop to those in the rear.

But then, having taken the cliff,
You will suddenly leave the field,
And disappear with the secret
Of helmets and cloaks unrevealed.

And I tomorrow, scattering dew,
Will stumble across a cannon-ball
And bring the tale into the room
As into an arsenal.

1927

98

To Anna Akhmatova

I think I can summon up words
    As pristine as those in your song.
But if I don't, I won't give a damn.
I don't care if I'm wrong.

I hear the murmur of wet roofs,
Faint eclogues of pavement and kerb.
A certain city, from the opening lines,
Resounds in every noun and verb.

Spring is all round, but one can't leave town.
The customer's deadline must be met.
Dawn glows and sews by the light of a lamp,
Her back unbending, her eyes wet.

Inhaling the calm of distant Ladoga,
She walks to the water with trembling legs.
Such strolls afford her no relief.
The dark canals smell of musty bags.

The wind bobs about like a walnut shell,
A hot wind flutters the glancing gleam
Of branches and stars, landmarks and lamps,
And the seamstress gazing upstream.

In different ways, the eyes can be sharp,
And images precise in different ways.
But a solution of terrible strength
Is out there under the white night's gaze.

And so I see your face and your glance.
The pillar of salt does not bring it to mind,
The one with which five years ago
You transfixed your fear of looking behind.

But from your first books, where the grains
Of keen prose crystallized, to the last,
Your eye, like the spark that makes the wire tremble,
Has forced events to vibrate with the past.

1928

TO A FRIEND

Do I not know that knocking on blackness,
  Darkness would never have tunnelled to light,
And am I a monster? Is not the happiness
Of millions more than a happy élite?

Do I not measure myself, stage by stage,
Against the Five-Year Plan's rise and fall?
But what can I do with my rib-cage
And the most tongue-tied fountain of all?

When seats are assigned to passion and vision
On the day of the great assembly,
Do not reserve a poet's position:
It is dangerous, if not empty.

1931

SECOND BIRTH

From WAVES

H ERE will be everything; all I have known,
   All that I live by, believe,
My aspirations and foundations,
And all that my senses perceive.

The waves of the sea are before me.
How many! Unthinkable millions.
They are legion. They sound in the minor key.
The surf is baking them like scones.

The shore is churned up, as by cattle.
They are legion. The herdsman noon
Has driven them to pasture
And stretched out behind a dune.

A herd of them, curling and rolling
The length and breadth of despondence,
My acts come stampeding towards me,
The crests of experience.

They are legion, they cannot be counted;
Incomplete, their meaning today;
But everything wears their succession,
As the song of the sea wears the spray.

1932

DEATH OF A POET

IMPOSSIBLE! Nonsense! they said,
   But heard it again from someone,
Everyone. Into the column
Of stopped time stepped the suburban
Villas of bank clerk and tradesman,
The backyards, trees, and overhead
Rooks, dazed with the blazing sun,
Haranguing their wives, damn them all,
And instructing each simpleton
To mind her own business from now on.
Faces, under the weight of loss,
Collapsed like drag-nets ripped across.

It was a day, a harmless one,
More harmless than many that led
To it. They crowded in the hall,
Lined up as for a firing squad.

You slept, with slander for a bed,
Slept, easy after all your action,
A handsome 22-year-old,
As your Tetraptych foretold.

You slept, the pillow under your head;
Slept, and at speed cutting through sleep,
Faster, faster, you took your place
Forever in the constellation
Of youthful legends. With one leap
You made it, were there in a trice.
Your shot, like an Etna, erupted
Among the foothills of cowardice.

1930

L OVING can be a heavy cross,
  But you are beautiful and straight
And the secret of your spell
Is as strong as the riddle of Fate.

In spring we hear the rustle of dreams,
A whisper as new truths appear.
You belong to that family.
Your meaning is selfless as air.

How easy to open one's eyes,
To shake the cant out of love
And live without rubbish in future.
That now is simple enough.

1931

M Y beauty, all your symmetry,
  All your dear essence long
To be transmuted to music
And beg to be rhyme, to be song.

And destiny dies in rhyme
And, as truth, there enters our time
The polyphony of the spheres.

And rhyme is not repetition
So much as a cloakroom token,
A ticket for a seat in the gods
In the posthumous rumble of sods.

And rhyme embodies that love
Which here is the source of pain;
A love which makes people frown
And purse their lips in disdain.

And rhyme is not repetition
But being granted admission
To exchange, as a coat for a token,
The weight of a body broken,
The fear of notoriety,
For the loud token of poetry.

My beauty, all your symmetry
And all your essence constrict
The breast and make me sing
And take the road – happily.

To you Polyclites prayed.
Your laws are for all to see.
Your laws are as old as the hills.
You have long been known to me.

1931

No one will be in the house
    But twilight. Just the same
Winter day in the gap
The gathered curtains frame.

Only swiftly beating wings
Of white flakes as they fall.
Only roofs and snow, and but
For roofs and snow – no one at all.

And frost again will start to sketch.
And I again will find despairs
Of last year whirling me back
To another winter's affairs.

And they again will sting me
With last year's guilt, the same,
Unexpiated. Lack of wood
Will cramp the window-frame.

Then suddenly the curtain
Will shudder at the door
And you will come in, like the future,
Making no sound on the floor.

And you will stand there wearing
Something white, no lace, no braid,
Something made from the fabric
From which snowflakes are made.

1931

WHILE we are climbing in the Caucasus
And, choking, the Kura drags
Itself through a gorge, in a cloud of gas,
To the Aragva crushed by crags;
And into August's marble firmament
Like gullets severed by the axe
The silhouettes of headless castles
Hold up their jagged necks.

While I throw back my head to count
The stumps of fortifications
That swim and drown in the lilac blue
Abyss of generations;
While from the elm groves' upper edge
The small curled shrubs continue,
What are you whispering, urging;
Caucasus, Caucasus, what should I do?

Embrace in a thousand outflankings,
What gives you your success?
And why do you laugh, hooding your eye
Under its eyelid, Caucasus?
When the dizzy heart misses a beat
And the mountain censers swing,
Do you think you somehow failed
To please me, my far darling?
And in the Alps, in distant Germany,
Where cliffs touch glasses and the touched rim rings
With echoes mistier than here,
Do you think you made a mess of things?

I am thrown into life, which carries the streams
Of the race down the stream of decades,
And to cut out my own is harder
Than cutting water with scissor blades.
Do not fear dreams, do not torment yourself.
Let be. I love, and think, and know.
Look, the rivers cannot be told apart
By life's transparent flow.

1931

If I had known that this is what happens,
 When I at first stood up and read;
That poetry is murderous,
Will strangle you and leave you dead;

I would have decided not
To play games with reality.
It all began so far away,
So long ago, so timidly.

But from an actor, age like Rome
Demands no cabaret routine –
Instead of a performance,
Irrevocable ruin.

When feeling dictates your lines,
You step out, like a slave, to pace
The stage, and here art stops,
And earth and fate breathe in your face.

1931

ON EARLY TRAINS

From SUMMER NOTES

I remember a dirty yard,
  Below it a wine cellar,
And seen from the attic
The mountains' apocrypha.

Clouds gather in a mass –
So massive the eyes quail –
But through them, single file,
Columns of scarecrows trail.

And holding out their hats
In chains of cloud, the files
Of glaciers dragged themselves
Along their day's slow miles.

At times, however,
Before the windows' eyes
The ridge of the Caucasus
Appeared otherwise.

The whole southern slope,
Silver-framed, would be looking
At windows and balconies
Where pancakes were cooking.

The gallery railings
Seemed lit by the same
Frost-fire that made altars
Beyond Aragva flame.

Annihilating time,
There soared the earth spirit
Of which we had such dreams,
Poor fibbers, in our garrets.

The tuff stretched out its arms
Where ancient blizzards swirled,
And knocked at eternal doors
With hands of the nether world.

1936

PINE TREES

IN grass, among wild balsam,
Dog-daisies and lilies, we lie,
Our arms thrown back behind us,
Our faces turned to the sky.

The grass in the pine-wood ride
Is impenetrably thick.
We look at each other and shift
A shoulder-blade or a cheek.

And there, for a time immortal,
We are numbered among the trees
And liberated from aches,
Disease, and the last disease.

With deliberate monotony,
Like blue oil from green eaves,
The sky pours down on the ground,
Dappling and staining our sleeves.

We share the repose of the pines
To the ant's accompaniment,
Inhaling the soporific
Incense-and-lemon scent.

So fiercely the fiery trunks
Leap up against the blue,
And under our resting heads
So long our hands rest too,

So broad our field of vision,
So docile all things on all sides,
That somewhere beyond the trunks
I imagine the surge of tides.

There waves are higher than branches,
And collapsing against the shore
They hurl down a hail of shrimps
From the ocean's turbulent floor.

And at evening, the sunset floats
On corks behind a trawler
And, shimmering with fish oil
And amber mist, grows smaller.

Twilight descends and slowly
The moon hides all trace of day
Beneath the black magic of water,
Beneath the white magic of spray.

And waves grow louder and higher
And the crowd at the floating café
Surrounds the pillar whose poster
Is a blur from far away.

1941

False Alarm

CATTLE trough and bucket,
  Confusion since dawn,
Rain squalls at sunset,
Damp evening coming on,

Tears choked down by dark sighs
In the dark hours before day,
A locomotive calling
From sixteen versts away

And early twilight
In backyard and garden,
And all those breakages ...
September's here again!

By day the breadth of autumn
Is scissored by the shriek
Of heartstruck anguish
From the churchyard by the creek.

And when the widow's sobbing
Is carried along the bank,
My heart goes out to her
And I see death point-blank.

I see from the hall window.
Today as every year,
My long delayed last day
At last arriving here.

And clearing a way
Downhill through horrible
Decaying yellow leaves,
Winter stares at my skull.

1941

Spring Again

VANISHED, the train. The embankment, black.
    How in the dark shall I find my way?
I don't recognize this place at all,
Though I've only been gone a day.
Echoes of iron have died on the sleepers.
Suddenly, what's that strange new racket?
All that confusion, chatter and clatter?
What the devil set them at it?

Where did I overhear snatches of this
Speech some time, was it last year?
Why, of course, it's the stream again
Springing out of the thicket here.
It's the mill-pond, as before,
Shaking the ice, breaking its chain,
Swelling and swirling. It's a new wonder.
As in the old days, it's Spring again.

She is here, she is here.
Magic and miracle are hers,
Hers the quilt jacket beyond the green willow,
Her back and hips, her plait and shoulders.
It's the Snow Maiden beside the bank,
It's about her that the crazy chatterbox
Babbles unceasingly in delirium
Tumbling over the gullies' rocks.

It's before her that, engulfing barriers,
Rapids are drowning in watery mist,
Nailed by the lamp of the hanging cascade,
Nailed with a hiss to the precipice.
It's the stream pouring, teeth chattering, numb,
Over the edge and into the pool,
Falling from that to a lower pool,
The speech of Spring flood is living's delirium.

                                            1941

WINTER APPROACHES

WINTER approaches. And once again
    The secret retreat of some bear
Will vanish under impassable mud
To a tearful child's despair.

Little huts will awaken in lakes
Reflecting their smoke like a path.
Encircled by autumn's cold slush,
Life-lovers will meet by the hearth.

Inhabitants of the stern North,
Whose roof is the open air,
'In this sign conquer' is written
On each inaccessible lair.

I love you, provincial retreats,
Off the map, off the road, past the farm.
The more thumbed and grubby the book,
The greater for me its charm.

Slow lines of lumbering carts,
You spell out an alphabet leading
From meadow to meadow. Your pages
Were always my favourite reading.

And suddenly here it is written
Again, in the first snow – the spidery
Cursive italic of sleigh runners –
A page like a piece of embroidery.

A silvery-hazel October.
Pewter shine since the frosts began.
Autumnal twilight of Chekhov,
Tchaikovsky and Levitan.

1943

THE OLD PARK

A small boy in a little bed.
    Savagely roars the storm.
Nines of cawing rooks fly off,
Scatter and re-form.

A doctor in a white coat
Was swabbing a stitched limb,
When the patient recognized
A childhood friend, his fathers' home.

Again he's in the old park.
Frosty mornings flash again,
And when they put on compresses,
Tears run down the outer pane.

Voices of this century
And visions of the last
Interweave as nurses' hands
Make his bandage fast.

People walk across the ward,
Doors bang in the corridor.
Gun batteries thud dully
Beyond the lake's far shore.

Lower sinks the setting sun.
It pierced the creek, withdrew,
And levelling its lance,
It runs the distance through.

And two minutes later, outside,
Into the craters flow
Wave on wave of emerald
As in a magic lantern show.

Pain attacks more fiercely,
Stronger the wind, fiercer the storm,
And nines of rooks, black nines of clubs
Scatter and re-form.

Turbulence contorts the limes,
Wind bends them to the ground,
And hearing the branches groan,
The patient forgets his wound.

Legends have aged the park.
Napoleon camped here,
And Samarin the Slavophil
Served and was buried near.

Descendant of the Decembrist,
Great-grandson of a heroine,
Here he shot at cawing crows
And overcame Latin.

If only he has strength enough,
The new enthusiast will
Revise his great-grandfather's works,
Edit the Slavophil.

He himself will write a play
Inspired by the war,
Thinks the patient lying there,
Hearing the forest roar.

The unimaginable course
Of life undreamt-of then
Will be plotted and revealed
By a provincial pen.

1943

FRESCO COME TO LIFE

AGAIN the shells were falling.
　　As on board ship, the cloud
And night sky over Stalingrad
Rocked in a plaster shroud.

Earth droned, as if in prayer
To ward off the shrieking shell,
And with its censer threw up smoke
And rubble where it fell.

Whenever, between fighting, he
Went round his company under fire,
A sense of strange familiarity
Haunted him like desire.

These hedgehog buildings, where could he
Have seen their bottomless holes before?
The evidence of past bombardments
Seemed fabulous and familiar.

What did it mean, the four-armed sign,
Enclosed in the pitch-black frame?
Of whom did they remind him,
The smashed floors and the flame?

And suddenly he saw his childhood,
His childhood, and the monastery; heard
The penitents, and in the garden
The nightingale and mocking-bird.

He gripped his mother with a son's hand,
And devils, fearing the archangel's spear,
Leaped from the chapel's sombre frescos
Into just such pits as here.

And the boy saw himself in armour.
Defending his mother in shining mail,
And fell upon the evil one
With its swastika-tipped tail.

And nearby in a mounted duel
Saint George shone down on the dragon,
And water-lilies studded the pond
And birds sang crazily on and on.

The fatherland, like the forest's voice,
A call in the wood and the wood's echo,
Beckoned with an alluring music
And smelt of budding birch and willow.

How he remembers those clearings
Now, when in pursuit he impales
And tramples enemy tanks
For all their fearful dragon scales.

He has crossed the frontiers of the world,
And the future, like the firmament,
Already rages, not a dream,
Approaching, and magnificent.

1944

POEMS FROM
DOCTOR ZHIVAGO

HAMLET

THE buzz subsides. I have come on stage.
   Leaning in an open door
I try to detect from the echo
What the future has in store.

A thousand opera-glasses level
The dark, point-blank, at me.
Abba, Father, if it be possible
Let this cup pass from me.

I love your preordained design
And am ready to play this role.
But the play being acted is not mine.
For this once let me go.

But the order of the acts is planned,
The end of the road already revealed.
Alone among the Pharisees I stand.
Life is not a stroll across a field.

1946

IN HOLY WEEK

STILL darkness, darkness everywhere.
   And still so early in the world,
Innumerable stars appear
And each so bright in the night air
That if the earth could count them there,
It would sleep through Easter, lulled
By chanted psalm and chanted prayer.

Still darkness, darkness everywhere.
The world has only just begun
And, like eternity, the square
Lies outstretched to the corner there,
And daybreak will not warm the air
Until a thousand years have run.

Still the earth is bare as bare,
And doesn't have a thing to wear
For ringing bells in the night air
Or echoing the choir out there.

From Maundy Thursday on,
Right up to Holy Saturday,
The water bores into the banks
And eddies on its way.

The wood is naked, unadorned,
And, for Christ's Passion, there
It stands, a congregation
Of silent pines at prayer.

But in the little open space
In town, the trees, all bare,
Are gathered before the church
And through its railings stare.

Their gaze is horrorstruck.
And there is the cause of their fear.
The gardens spill as fences break,
The earth's foundations shake.
God is being buried here.

And they see light at the holy gates,
Low candles that illuminate
Black robes and streaming cheeks – the crowd
That, now emerging, elevates
Christ's cross and bannered shroud,
And birches at the outer gates
Make way for them and bow.

The procession goes the rounds
Of the monastery bounds
And brings back from the pavement
Spring, a babble of spring sounds,
Air tasting of the sacrament
And smelling of the ground.

And March dispenses flakes of snow
To cripples in the portico,
As if somebody who had borne
A reliquary raised the lid
And scattered every shred.

And singing lasts until the dawn,
When, having wept to their hearts' content,
Gospel and psalm, all passion spent,
More quietly retreat
Along the lamplit street.

But fur and flesh will hold their breath
At midnight, hearing spring's prediction
That wind and weather change direction,
And death may then be put to death
By the power of Resurrection.

1946

FOUL WAYS IN SPRING

THE sunset blaze was burning down.
  Along a muddy forest ride,
A horseman jogged towards a farm
On a Ural mountainside.

The horse was in a lather
And the horseshoes' splashing clatter
Was echoed back along the track
By streams' torrential chatter.

But when the rider dropped the reins
And went at walking pace,
The spring thaw-water galloped by
And bellowed in his face.

There was laughter, there was crying,
Flint splintered stones and loam,
And tree-stumps torn up by the roots
Collapsed into dizzy foam.

Against the blaze of sunset,
That charred far branches as it fell,
A nightingale was raging
Insistent as a tocsin bell.

And where the willow by the gulley
Bent down and trailed her widow's veil,
He played his flute of seven oaks
Like the Robber Nightingale.

What did his ardent song foretell?
Catastrophe or mad desire?
At whom, from coverts under cover,
Did he direct his rapid fire?

It seemed the Demon of the Woods,
Emerging from some hiding hole
Of convicts on the run, would meet
A partisan patrol.

The earth and sky, the field and forest
Were listening for this rare strain
Combining measured portions
Of madness, happiness, and pain.

c. 1948

THE WIND

I am dead, but you are living.
   And the wind, moaning and grieving,
Rocks the house and the forest,
Not one pine after another
But further than the furthest
Horizon all together,
Like boat-hulls and bowsprits
In an unruffled anchorage,
Rocked not from high spirits
Or out of aimless rage,
But with a sad heart seeking
Words for your cradle-song.

1953

HOPS

BENEATH the willow, wound round with ivy,
    We take cover from the worst
Of the storm, with a greatcoat round
Our shoulders and my hands around your waist.

I've got it wrong. That isn't ivy
Entwined in the bushes round
The wood, but hops. You intoxicate me!
Let's spread the greatcoat on the ground.

1953

WEDDING

GUESTS across the cobbled court,
    Making for the bride's place
And an all-night party, brought
An accordion in its case.

On the landlord's side
Of the green-baize door
The babble of voices
Died down about four.

But at daylight, scattering sleep –
Oh, the longing to sleep more –
Burst out the accordion
Back from the bride's door.

Once more the musician
Conjured from his squeezebox there
Clapping hands and flashing beads,
All the fun of the fair.

And again, again, again,
Once again the gipsy lilt
Burst in on the sleepers
Snug beneath their quilt.

And a woman, white as snow,
Through the whistling and singing
Once more like a peacock
Danced with hips swinging,

Swaying head and swaying hand
Swaying with her frock,
Danced over the courtyard,
Peacock, peacock, peacock.

Suddenly the dancers'
Racket grew quieter,
Stamping feet made off,
Sank like stones through water.

As the noisy yard woke up,
Echoes of men haggling
Merged with womens' gossip
And children giggling.

Into the enormous sky
Blue feather, grey feather,
Pigeons from the pigeonlofts
Spiralled up together

Like a waking afterthought
Hurriedly sent express
With best wishes for a long
Lifetime's happiness.

Life is just a moment's pulse,
Just a swift dissolving
Of ourselves in everyone,
Like a wedding gift.

Just a wedding, through wide windows
Rushing in together;
Just a song, just a dream,
Just a blue-grey feather.

1954

Autumn

I have let my household disperse,
  My dear ones have long been apart,
And a familiar loneliness
Fills all of nature and all my heart.

Here I am with you in the lodge.
No one walks through the woods these days.
As in the old song, undergrowth
Has almost hidden the forest ways.

Forlornly, the timber walls
Look down on the two of us here.
We did not promise to leap obstacles,
We shall fall at last in the clear.

We shall sit down from one till three,
You with embroidery, I deep
In a book, and at dawn shall not see
When we kiss each other to sleep.

More richly and more recklessly,
Leaves, leaves, give tongue and whirl away,
Fill yesterday's cup of bitterness
With the sadness of today.

Impulse, enchantment, beauty!
Let's dissolve in September wind
And enter the rustle of autumn!
Be still, or go out of your mind!

As the coppice lets slip its leaves,
You let your dress slip rustling down
And throw yourself into my arms
In your silk-tasselled dressing gown.

You are my joy on the brink
Of disaster, when life becomes
A plague, and beauty is daring,
And draws us into each other's arms.

c. 1947

WINTER NIGHT

SNOW, snow, all the world over,
  Snow to the world's end swirling,
A candle was burning on the table,
A candle burning.

As midges swarming in summer
Fly to the candle flame,
The snowflakes swarming outside
Flew at the window frame.

The blizzard etched on the window
Frosty patterning.
A candle was burning on the table,
A candle burning.

The lighted ceiling carried
A shadow frieze:
Entwining hands, entwining feet,
Entwining destinies.

And two little shoes dropped,
Thud, from the mattress.
And candle wax like tears dropped
On an empty dress.

And all was lost in a tunnel
Of grey snow churning.
A candle was burning on the table,
A candle burning.

And when a draught flattened the flame,
Temptation blazed
And like a fiery angel raised
Two cross-shaped wings.

All February the snow fell
And sometimes till morning
A candle was burning on the table,
A candle burning.

1948

AUGUST

THE sun called me bright and early –
  As promised, I was not misled –
A slanting shaft of saffron
Extending from curtain to bed.

It overpainted with warm ochre
The settlement, the nearby wood,
My bed, wet pillow, and the edge
Of the wall where the bookcase stood.

And then I remembered the reason
The pillow was damp at the corner.
I had dreamed that at my funeral
You walked through the wood, mourner by mourner.

You walked in a crowd, in ones and twos,
And suddenly someone remembered
That that this was the sixth of August,
The Transfiguration of our Lord.

On that day from Mount Tabor
A light without flame should rise
And, clear as a sign from heaven,
Autumn attract all eyes.

You went through the beggarly, bare,
Sparse, trembling alder grove
Among the crimson graveyard trees
That glowed as if fresh from the stove.

The sky kept solemn company
With the grieving trees' hushed tops,
And distance responded to distance
In the long crowing of cocks.

And death stood there, like an official,
Between the headstones in the grove,
And stared at me as though to gauge
The right dimensions of the grave.

And every bystander could sense
A calm voice speaking in his head.
It was my once prophetic voice,
Untouched by corruption, that said:

'Farewell, azure of Transfiguration,
Gold Second Sunday of our Saviour,
Assuage with one last feminine caress
The bitterness of the appointed hour.

Farewell, decades of deprivation.
We part, my love, who would not yield
To onslaughts of humiliation!
I am your battlefield.

Farewell, extended wing, the free
Ascent of imagination,
The whole world imaged in the word,
The miracles of creation.'

1953

MAGDALENE

EACH night brings back my demon,
  My fee for services rendered.
The memories of sin crowd in
Like vampires sucking at my heart,
Remembering how I surrendered
To men's desires, a crazy tart
Only at home on the boulevard.

A few minutes more and then
The lips of the grave will meet.
But first I will go as far
As I can, and break open
My life, Lord, at Your feet
Like an alabaster jar.

Oh, where now would I be,
My Teacher and Redeemer,
If every night eternity
Were not ensconced in my flat
And waiting like a customer,
Entangled in my net?

But what is the meaning of sin and death
And hell, when everyone can see
Me grafted indissolubly
To You, as a cutting to a tree,
In my immeasurable grief?

And, Jesus, when I press
Your feet against my knees,
Perhaps I am learning already
To hug the square shaft of a cross
And, swooning, I prepare Your body
For other oils than these.

                              1949

137

The Garden of Gethsemane

Indifferently, the glimmer of stars
Lit up the turning in the road.
The road went round the Mount of Olives,
Below it the Kedron flowed.

The meadow suddenly stopped half-way.
The Milky Way went on from there.
The grey and silver olive trees
Were trying to march into thin air.

There was a garden at the meadow's end.
And leaving the disciples by the wall,
He said: 'My soul is sorrowful unto death,
Tarry ye here, and watch with Me awhile.'

Without a struggle He renounced
Omnipotence and miracles
As if they had been borrowed things,
And now He was a mortal among mortals.

The night's far reaches seemed a region
Of nothing and annihilation. All
The universe was uninhabited.
There was no life outside the garden wall.

And looking at those dark abysses,
Empty and endless, bottomless deeps,
He prayed the Father, in a bloody sweat,
To let this cup pass from His lips.

Assuaging mortal agony with prayer,
He left the garden. By the road he found
Disciples, overcome by drowsiness,
Asleep spreadeagled on the ground.

He wakened them: 'The Lord has deemed you worthy
To live in My time. Is it worthiness
To sleep in the hour when the Son of Man
Must give Himself into the hands of sinners?'

And hardly had he spoken, when a mob
Of slaves, a ragged multitude, appeared
With torches, swords, and Judas at their head
Shaping a traitor's kiss behind his beard.

Peter with his sword resisted them
And severed one man's ear. But then he heard
These words: 'The sword is no solution.
Put up your blade, man, in its scabbard.

Could not My Father instantly send down
Legions of angels in one thunderous gust?
Before a hair of my head was touched,
My enemies would scatter like the dust.

But now the book of life has reached a page
Most precious and most holy. What the pen
Foretold in Scripture here must be fulfilled.
Let prophecy come to pass. Amen.

The course of centuries is like a parable
And, passing, can catch fire. Now, in the name
Of its dread majesty, I am content
To suffer and descend into the tomb.

I shall descend and on the third day rise,
And as the river rafts float into sight,
Towards My Judgement like a string of barges
The centuries will float out of the night.'

1949

WHEN
THE WEATHER
CLEARS

IN everything I want to reach
  The very essence:
In work, in seeking a way,
In passion's turbulence.

The essence of past days
And where they start,
Foundations, roots,
The very heart.

Always catching the thread
Of actions, histories,
To live, to think, to feel, to love,
To make discoveries.

If only I could do it
After a fashion,
I should compose eight lines
On the properties of passion,

On lawlessnesses, sins,
Pursuits, alarms,
On unexpectednesses,
Elbows, palms.

I should deduce its principles,
Its laws proclaim,
Repeating the initials
Of name after name.

I should plant out my stanzas.
And flowering limes,
Their veins astir with sap,
Would bloom in lines.

I should have mint and roses
Breathing there –
Sedge, meadows, haymaking,
And thundrous air.

So Chopin once enclosed
The plenitude
Of farmsteads, parks, groves, graves
In his *Etudes*.

The torment and delight
Of triumph so
Achieved tightens the bowstring
Bending the bow.

1956

July

A phantom roams through the house.
   There are footsteps in upstairs rooms.
All day, shades flit through the attic.
Through the house a goblin roams.

He loafs about, gets in the way,
He interferes and causes trouble,
Creeps up to the bed in a dressing gown,
And pulls the cloth off the table.

He does not wipe his feet at the door,
But whirls in with the draught, unseen,
And hurls the curtain to the ceiling
Like a prima ballerina.

Who can this irritating oaf,
This ghost, this phantom be?
Of course, it is our summer guest,
Our visitor on the spree.

For all his little holiday
We let him have the whole house.
July with his tempestuous air
Has rented rooms from us.

July, who brings in thistledown
And burs that cling to his clothes;
July, who treats all windows as doors,
And sprinkles his talk with oaths.

Untidy urchin of the steppe,
Smelling of lime-trees, grass, and rye,
Beet-tops, and fragrant fennel,
Meadowsweet breath of July.

1956

HAYRICKS

VERMILION dragonflies dart,
   Bees bumble on all sides,
Farm women laugh from the cart,
Harvesters pass with scythes.

While fine weather holds,
They turn the hay with rakes
And build it before sunset
Into house-high ricks.

A rick at dusk resembles
An inn where night can stay
And lie down to sleep
On clover and mown hay.

When darkness thins, near morning,
The rick looms like a barn
In which the passing moon
Has burrowed down till dawn.

At first light, cart after cart
Rolls through dim meadows where
The day gets out of bed
With dust and hay in his hair.

At noon, the heights are blue once more.
Again the ricks are strung
Like clouds, again like anisette
The earth is fragrant and strong.

1957

WHEN THE WEATHER CLEARS

THE wide lake is a platter.
   Behind it, cloudy masses
Are heaped in a grim pile
Of glaciers and crevasses.

Whenever the light changes
The wood is painted out.
One minute, all on fire;
The next, all under soot.

When after rainy days
Clouds part, blue glances pass,
How festive looks the sky between,
How jubilant the grass!

The sun is poured over earth,
Distances wind swept clean.
The green of leaves shines through,
As in a stained-glass scene.

Thus, paintings in church windows,
The hermits, saints, and tsars
In bright crowns of insomnia,
Stare outward to the stars.

As if the open earth were nave,
And from its stained-glass tiers
The distant echo of a choir
Came sometimes to my ears.

I tremble, Nature, world,
The monstrance of creation,
And weeping joyfully attend
Your long Communion.

1956

THE WIND
(Four fragments about Blok)

WHO is to be honoured and living
And who without honour and dead
Nobody knows in our country
Till Establishment yes-men have said.

Should Pushkin be honoured or not?
I dare say that no one could tell
Were it not for their doctoral theses
That lighten our darkness so well.

But Blok, thank heaven, is different,
Luckily a different case.
He did not come down from Sinai
To put us in our place.

His fame, his eternity depend
On no curricula, no schools.
He was not made by human hand
To be stuffed down our throats by fools.

*

He is free as the wind, the wind
That in the avenue used to scream
When still the postillion galloped
On the front horse of the team

And grandfather was still alive,
A Jacobin, crystal-souled,
Whose whirlwind grandson
Was cast in the same mould.

That wind, which cut through his ribs
And penetrated his soul,
Over the years entered his poems
To sing of fair weather and foul.

That wind enters everywhere – house,
Trees, village, and rain; it is there
In the Third Book of poems,
In 'The Twelve', in death – everywhere.

*

As far as the eye can see
River and meadow stretch away.
On all sides confused activity,
The bustle of making hay.
The mowers by the water's edge
See nothing beyond their swathe.
The mowing went to Blok's head
And the young squire snatched up a scythe,
Lashed out, just missing a hedgehog,
And sliced two adders in half.

But he hadn't finished his homework.
'You slacker!' they scolded the truant.
Childhood! Boredom of blackboard and chalk!
Songs of farm-girl and servant!

But clouds from the east roll in
Towards evening. North and south darken.
A savage unseasonal wind
Whirls down, launching a sudden
Assault on the scythes, on the sedge,
The rushes by the river's edge.

Childhood! Boredom of blackboard and chalk!
Songs of farm-girl and servant!
As far as the eye can see
River and meadow stretch away.

*

The sharpened horizon threatens
A contused twilight, that shows
Lacerations bloody as those
Unhealed on the mowers' shins.

The sky's countless gashes are omens
Of storm and disaster
And the air in the marshes smells
Of iron, rust, and water.

Over wood, over road, over gully,
Over village, and over farm
Forked lightning inscribes the clouds
With prophecies of storm.

But when the sky over the city
Surrounds it with a rusty band,
The state is about to be shaken,
A hurricane shadows the land.

Blok saw the writing on the sky.
The heavens foretold him it meant
Foul weather, a thunderstorm,
A great cyclone imminent.

Blok waited for this convulsion.
Its contours are etched in flames,
With dread and desire for its outcome,
In his life and the lines of his poems.

1956

SNOW IS FALLING

SNOW is falling, snow is falling.
  Reaching for the storm's white stars,
Petals of geraniums stretch
Beyond the window bars.

Snow is falling, all is chaos,
Everything is in the air,
The angle of the crossroads,
The steps of the back stair.

Snow is falling, not like flakes
But as if the firmament
In a coat with many patches
Were making its descent.

As if, from the upper landing,
Looking like a lunatic,
Creeping, playing hide-and-seek,
The sky stole from the attic.

Because life does not wait,
Turn, and you find Christmas here.
And a moment after that
It's suddenly New Year.

Snow is falling, thickly, thickly.
Keeping step, stride for stride,
No less quickly, nonchalantly,
Is that time, perhaps,
Passing in the street outside?

And perhaps year follows year
Like the snowflakes falling
Or the words that follow here?

Snow is falling, snow is falling,
Snow is falling, all is chaos:
The whitened ones who pass,
The angle of the crossroads,
The dazed plants by the glass.

1957

AFTER THE BLIZZARD

AFTER the blizzard has dwindled,
    Tranquillity comes here today.
I listen to children's voices
Beyond the river at play.

No, surely, I must be mistaken,
I'm blind, I'm on the wrong track.
Like a dead white woman of plaster
Winter lies flat on her back.

The sky is admiring the moulding
Of eyelids forever pressed shut.
Snow covers everything: yard and twig
And the tree's most diminutive shoot.

The river ice, crossing and platform,
The forest, embankment and track
Have been cast in immaculate forms
With no jutting corner or crack.

At night, when I can't get to sleep,
Revelation leaps up from the sofa
To fit the whole world in a page,
To accommodate all in a stanza;

As tree stumps and tree roots are sculpted,
And the riverside bushes below,
To build the roofs' seascape on paper,
The whole town, the whole world in snow.

c. 1956

It Has All Been Fulfilled

THE roads have turned to porridge.
  Across the fields I trudge.
I mash up icy mud to dough,
I plod through fudgelike sludge.

A blue-jay flies between
The wood's bare birches, scolding.
The wood, like an unfinished house,
Holds up its scaffolding.

I see between its arches
My future life revealed.
It all, to the last particle,
Has been accomplished and fulfilled.

I take my time in the wood.
Snow layers lie heavily.
The blue-jay's echo will answer me,
The world make way for me.

Where snow has thawed and earth
And sodden loam show through,
A bird is chirping mutedly
Every second or two.

The wood gives ear, as if
A musical box were played;
Repeats the bird's chirp hollowly
And waits for it to fade.

I hear, then, from the boundary fence,
Three miles off, crunching hooves
And footsteps, drips falling from trees,
And snow flopping off roofs.

1958

NOBEL PRIZE

LIKE a beast in a pen, I'm cut off
  From my friends, freedom, the sun,
But the hunters are gaining ground.
I've nowhere else to run.

Dark wood and the bank of a pond,
Trunk of a fallen tree.
There's no way forward, no way back.
It's all up with me.

Am I gangster or murderer?
Of what crime do I stand
Condemned? I made the whole world weep
At the beauty of my land.

Even so, one step from my grave,
I believe that cruelty, spite,
The powers of darkness will in time
Be crushed by the spirit of light.

The beaters in a ring close in
With the wrong prey in view.
I've nobody at my right hand,
Nobody faithful and true.

And with such a noose on my throat
I should like for one second
My tears to be wiped away
By someone at my right hand.

1959

Notes

Many of Pasternak's early poems were extensively revised in subsequent editions. Unless otherwise indicated, our translations follow the versions printed in the Biblioteka Poeta (BP) edition (Moscow–Leningrad, 1965). Poems not included in this edition (for the most part, poems from *Doctor Zhivago* with overtly Christian themes) have been translated from the standard Western editions. Dates of composition have been supplied where these are known. For fuller comment on several of the poems, see the chapter on Pasternak in Peter France, *Poets of Modern Russia* (Cambridge, 1982).

(p. 47) IT'S FEBRUARY. WEEPING, TAKE INK
This and the next two poems come from Pasternak's first, Futurist collection, *Twin in the Clouds* (1914).

(p. 48) VENICE
This is the first version of the poem. BP gives a considerably revised text. For Pasternak's comments on 'Venice', see Introduction, p. 22.

(p. 53) WINTER SKY
This and the next five poems come from Pasternak's second collection, *Over the Barriers* (1917), of which he subsequently wrote that its principal characteristics were 'objectivity of theme and the rapid pictorial representation of movement'. The last line refers to the punishment of forgers by pouring molten metal into their mouths.

(p. 53) THE URALS FOR THE FIRST TIME
Pasternak spent many months during the First World War in the Urals. See Introduction, p. 23.

(p. 54) SPRING
This is the first of a cycle of three poems, originally entitled 'Poetry in Spring'.

(p. 56) IMPROVISATION
On Pasternak and music, see Introduction, p. 18.

(p. 56) MARBURG
This is one of the most frequently and extensively revised of all Pasternak's poems (see Introduction, p. 30). The text translated here is a late version given in the three-volume Michigan edition of Pasternak's work edited by G. P. Struve and B. A. Filippov (Michigan, 1961); the BP version is considerably longer.
    Pasternak spent the summer term of 1912 at Marburg, studying philosophy under Hermann Cohen. The poem alludes both to a love affair and to the poet's acceptance of his vocation; see Introduction, p. 18, and for a fuller account, Pasternak's autobiographical work *Safe Conduct*, Part 2.

(p. 61) ABOUT THESE POEMS
This is the second poem in Pasternak's most important early book of poetry, *My Sister Life*, which was inspired both by personal experiences and by the excitement of the period between the two revolutions of 1917 (see Introduction, p. 25). The book was dedicated to the Russian Romantic poet, Mikhail Lermontov (1814–1841). Pasternak was hostile to what he called romanticism, but he explained in a letter of 1958 to an American translator, Eugene M. Kayden, that he saw in Lermontov not so much romanticism as 'modern personal biographical realism and the foreshadowing of our modern poetry and prose'. Darial is the name of a narrow gorge in the Caucasus, which features prominently in Lermontov's poetry.

(p. 62) MY SISTER, LIFE, IS TODAY OVERFLOWING
This translation follows the Michigan edition, which differs from BP in the third stanza. Kamyshin is a town in southern Russia, near the Volga. The third bell is a signal for the train's departure.

(p. 64) MIRROR
Originally entitled 'Myself'. Our translation follows later versions of the poem which omit three stanzas of the first version (printed in BP).

(p. 66) FROM SUPERSTITION
The first line refers to a brand of matches which had a picture of an orange on the box.

(p. 67) OARS CROSSED
The version translated here is taken from a 1957 revision and is different from that printed in BP.

(p. 67) SPRING RAIN
Here the reference to the political situation is more obvious than in most of the poems of *My Sister Life*. Kerensky was the influential Minister of Justice in the Provisional Government set up in March 1917 after the abdication of Tsar Alexander III.

(p. 68) MALADIES OF THE EARTH
The Klyazma is a river in central Russia, flowing into the Oka. Niagara reads in the original Imatra, the name of a waterfall in Finland.

(p. 70) SPARROW HILLS
The Sparrow Hills are on a bend of the Moscow River, near the present site of Moscow University. In 1917 they were on the outskirts of the city.

(p. 71) STEPPE
Kerch is a town in the Crimea.

(p. 73) LET WORDS DROP, AS RESIN
The epigraph is taken from another poem in *My Sister Life*. Jagiello and Jadwiga were the Grand Duke of Lithuania and the Polish queen whose marriage laid the foundation for Polish–Lithuanian unity in the fourteenth century.

(pp. 77–8) *From* THEME AND VARIATIONS
There are in fact a total of six variations on the original theme, which evokes the figure of the poet Pushkin, one of whose ancestors was 'Peter the Great's Nigger', more exactly an Abyssinian Engineer-General. There is a stone Sphinx on the waterfront in Petersburg. The 'Prophet' mentioned in 'Variation 3' is one of Pushkin's most famous and grandiose poems.

(p. 79) JANUARY 1919
This poem comes from a small cycle entitled 'Illness'. The hard times of the first revolutionary winters are evoked in *Doctor Zhivago*.

(p. 85) MUTINY AT SEA
The title suggests both a (natural) storm and a (human) mutiny. This poem is one of a group of long historical poems written in 1925 to commemorate the Revolution of 1905. Eisenstein's film *Battleship Potemkin*, which resembles Pasternak's poem in many ways, was part of the same celebration. The place names are all in the Black Sea, where the mutiny took place; Matyushenko was one of the leaders. Port Arthur is the Russian port which was captured by the Japanese in the Russo–Japanese War of 1904–5.

(p. 96) LILY OF THE VALLEY
Uglich is the city where Dmitry, son of Ivan the Terrible, was murdered in 1591. See Pushkin's *Boris Godunov*.

(p. 97) NIGHT VIOLET
The plant called the night violet is a member of the orchid family whose scent is strongest at night. Spoon bait is a shiny form of bait resembling a small fish.

(p. 98) GATHERING STORM
The historical reference here is to the wars between Peter the Great and the Swedish armies under Charles XII, which ended with the battle of Poltava in 1709.

(p. 99) TO ANNA AKHMATOVA
Pasternak is here evoking Akhmatova's city of Petersburg, so different from his own Moscow. The penultimate stanza is a reference to her poem of 1923 on the subject of Lot's wife, which ends with the lines:

> Only my heart will never forget her
> Who gave her life for a single glance.

Ladoga is a large lake near Petersburg/Leningrad.

(p. 100) TO A FRIEND
For the political context of this poem see the Introduction, p. 30. The final line is ambiguous; it can be read either 'It is dangerous unless it is left empty' or (more probably) 'It is dangerous, not to say empty'.

(p. 103) *From* WAVES
The sequence 'Waves', which opens the collection *Second Birth* (1932), reflects Pasternak's visit to Georgia with Zinaida Neuhaus in 1931; on this and the idea of second birth see the Introduction, pp. 30–2.

(p. 104) DEATH OF A POET

This poem is a reaction to the death of the poet Vladimir Mayakovsky, who shot himself as a result of political pressures and personal unhappiness. It was originally considerably longer. The first published version contained eight lines that were subsequently omitted, and there was also a final stanza which was never published, but whose absence was indicated in the first publication by the title 'A Fragment' and by a line of dots at the end of the poem. The omitted stanza was a satirical attack on the reactions of literary circles to the suicide.

The title 'Death of a Poet' is also that of Lermontov's famous invective about the death of Pushkin. The 'Tetraptych' is Mayakovsky's first long poem, *Cloud in Trousers*, where the poet presents himself as 'handsome, 22-year-old'.

(p. 105) LOVING CAN BE A HEAVY CROSS

This and the next poem are addressed to Zinaida Neuhaus, who became Pasternak's second wife in 1934.

(p. 106) NO ONE WILL BE IN THE HOUSE

'Lack of wood' is a reference to the shortage of fuel in Moscow at this time.

(p. 107) WHILE WE ARE CLIMBING IN THE CAUCASUS

The second part of the third stanza is addressed to Pasternak's first wife, who had left for the West earlier in 1931. The Aragva and the Kura are both rivers in the Caucasus.

(p. 113) *From* SUMMER NOTES

Pasternak wrote very little poetry between 1931 and 1940 (see Introduction, pp. 33–5). This is one of a group of poems about Georgia published in the journal *Novy Mir* in the autumn of 1936.

(p. 114) PINE TREES

This and the next two poems belong to a sequence entitled 'Peredelkino', the writers' village just outside Moscow, in which Pasternak settled in 1936. He continued to live there for most of the year until the time of his death, and the village provides the setting for many of the lyric poems in his later collections.

(p. 118) WINTER APPROACHES

Levitan was a famous Russian landscape painter of the nineteenth century.

(p. 119) THE OLD PARK

This and the next poem belong to the sequence 'War Poems'. The park referred to here is the estate in Peredelkino, which had formerly belonged to the Slavophil writer Yury Samarin (1819–1876) – see Pasternak's *Essay in Autobiography*, Chapter 4. The 'provincial pen' of the last stanza is an allusion to Pasternak's search for a more ordinary and unpretentious language in his later writing.

(p. 125) HAMLET

This is the first of the poems which make up the final chapter of the novel *Doctor Zhivago*. It should be remembered that all the Zhivago poems are presented as the work of the hero of the novel, although at the same time they clearly belong to Pasternak (see Chapters 12 and 13 of Henry Gifford's *Pasternak*, Cambridge University Press, 1977).

It seems that the immediate reference in this poem is to the big public poetry readings which were and are a feature of Soviet literary life (see also the poem beginning 'If I had known'). But more generally, the sacrificial note sounded here refers to Pasternak's determination to tell the truth as he saw it whatever the cost. He had translated Shakespeare's tragedy into Russian and took a heroic view of the character of the prince (see Anna Kay France, *Boris Pasternak's Translations of Shakespeare*, Berkeley, 1978). Like 'In Holy Week', 'August', 'Magdalene', and 'The Garden of Gethsemane', this poem has never been published in the Soviet Union, but thousands of people know it by heart and it was spoken at the poet's funeral.

The final line is a proverbial saying.

(p. 128) FOUL WAYS IN SPRING

This poem seems to relate to Section 16 of Chapter 9 of *Doctor Zhivago*. The Robber Nightingale of Stanza 6 is a sinister figure from folk epic, who whistled on a flute made of seven oak trees and was challenged and defeated by the legendary hero Ilya of Murom.

(p. 130) WEDDING

In its rhythm, this poem resembles the *chastushka* or popular factory song.

(p. 133) WINTER NIGHT

The image of the candle burning at a window is a central one in *Doctor Zhivago*.

(p. 135) AUGUST

The Transfiguration, also referred to as the Second Sunday of our Saviour, is one of the major festivals of the Orthodox church. It commemorates the occasion when Christ took three of his disciples up on to Mount Tabor and appeared transfigured before them – 'his face did shine as the sun, and his raiment was white as the light' (*Matthew* 17:2).

(p. 137) MAGDALENE

This is the first of two poems which are spoken by Mary Magdalene.

(p. 138) THE GARDEN OF GETHSEMANE

This, the last of the Zhivago poems, takes up the theme of the Mount of Olives which is announced in the opening poem, 'Hamlet', thus completing the sacrificial cycle.

(p. 143) IN EVERYTHING I WANT TO REACH

Pasternak's final book of poems, known under the title *When the Weather Clears*, dates from the years 1956 to 1959, when the writing of *Doctor Zhivago* was finished. This is the first poem in the book and declares the poet's attachment to 'subjective-biographical realism'. He also wrote an article on Chopin which affirms the same position.

(p. 147) THE WIND

Alexander Blok (1880–1921), one of Russia's greatest poets, was a major influence on Pasternak, and his significance is stressed at several points in *Doctor Zhivago*, and in the *Essay on Autobiography*, Chapter 3 (see above, Introduction, p. 21). This cycle of poems refers to various scenes in Blok's family life. His grandfather,

Andrey Beketov, was the liberal-minded Rector of St Petersburg University, and the family spent most summers in the country outside Moscow. Blok's third book of poems is full of premonitions of disaster, and 'The Twelve', written in 1918, is his fierce and ambiguous cantata of the Revolution. On Blok see Avril Pyman, *The Life of Aleksandr Blok* (2 vols. Oxford, 1979–80) and A. Blok, *The Twelve and Other Poems*, translated by Jon Stallworthy and Peter France (Eyre & Spottis-woode, 1970).

(p. 154) NOBEL PRIZE
On the Nobel Prize affair, see the Introduction, p. 40. This poem originally ended on a more positive note after the fourth stanza. The final two stanzas were an afterthought added to the manuscript on a separate piece of paper; it is not certain that they should be retained – or indeed that Pasternak would have wanted this poem to be published. On the personal background to the poem, see Olga Ivinskaya's *A Captive of Time*, pp. 330–32, and note 43.